1

GOLDEN WORDS UPON GOLDEN WORDS...FOR EVERY MUSLIM.

"Imaam al-Barbahaaree, may Allaah have mercy upon him said:

May Allaah have mercy upon you! Examine carefully the speech of everyone you hear from in your time particularly. So do not act in haste and do not enter into anything from it until you ask and see: Did any of the Companions of the Prophet, may Allaah's praise and salutations be upon him, speak about it, or did any of the scholars? So if you find a narration from them about it, cling to it, do not go beyond it for anything and do not give precedence to anything over it and thus fall into the Fire.

Explanation by Sheikh Saaleh al-Fauzaan, may Allaah preserve him:

'Do not be hasty in accepting as correct what you may hear from the people especially in these later times. As now there are many who speak about so many various matters, issuing rulings and ascribing to themselves both knowledge and the right to speak. This is especially the case after the emergence and spread of new modern day media technologies.

Such that everyone now can speak and bring forth that which is in truth worthless; by this meaning words of no true value - speaking about whatever they wish in the name of knowledge and in the name of the religion of Islaam. It has even reached the point that you find the people of misguidance and the members of the various groups of misguidance and deviance from the religion speaking as well. Such individuals have now become those who speak in the name of the religion of Islaam through means such as the various satellite television channels. Therefore be very cautious!

It is upon you oh Muslim, and upon you oh student of knowledge individually, to verify matters and not rush to embrace everything and anything you may hear. It is upon you to verify the truth of what you hear, asking, 'Who else also makes this same statement or claim?', 'Where did this thought or concept originate or come from?', 'Who is its reference or source authority?'. Asking what are the evidences which support it from within the Book and the Sunnah? And inquiring where has the individual who is putting this forth studied and taken his knowledge from? From who has he studied the knowledge of Islaam?

Each of these matters requires verification through inquiry and investigation, especially in the present age and time. As it is not every speaker who should rightly be considered a source of knowledge, even if he is well spoken and eloquent, and can manipulate words captivating his listeners. Do not be taken in and accept him until you are aware of the degree and scope of what he possesses of knowledge and understanding. As perhaps someone's words may be few, but possess true understanding, and perhaps another will have a great deal of speech yet he is actually ignorant to such a degree that he doesn't actually posses anything of true understanding. Rather he only has the ability to enchant with his speech so that the people are deceived. Yet he puts forth the perception that he is a scholar, that he is someone of true understanding and comprehension, that he is a capable thinker, and so forth. Through such means and ways he is able to deceive and beguile the people, taking them away from the way of truth.

Therefore what is to be given true consideration is not the amount of the speech put forth or that one can extensively discuss a subject. Rather the criterion that is to be given consideration is what that speech contains within it of sound authentic knowledge, what it contains of the established and transmitted principles of Islaam. As perhaps a short or brief statement which is connected to or has a foundation in the established principles can be of greater benefit than a great deal of speech which simply rambles on, and through hearing you don't actually receive very much benefit from.

This is the reality which is present in our time; one sees a tremendous amount of speech which only possesses within it a small amount of actual knowledge. We see the presence of many speakers yet few people of true understanding and comprehension.' "

[The eminent major scholar Sheikh Saaleh al-Fauzaan, may Allaah preserve him- 'A Valued Gift for the Reader Of Comments Upon the Book Sharh as-Sunnah', page 102-103]

My Home, My Path
Pocket Edition

1.

Islamic
Rulings

Translated & Compiled By
Umm Mujaahid Khadijah Bint Lacina
al-Amreekiyyah as-Salafiyyah

Table of Contents

This pocket edition is a selection taken from the larger book:

My Home, My Path

A Comprehensive Source Book For Today's Muslim Woman Discussing Her Essential Role & Contribution To The Establishment of Islaam – Taken From The Words Of The People Of Knowledge

Collected and Translated by
Umm Mujaahid Khadijah Bint Lacina
al-Amreekiyyah

|Available: **Now** ¦ pages: **420+** ¦
price: (Soft cover) **$22.50**
(Hard cover) **$29.50**
(eBook) **$9.99**]

About the Compiler & Translator

The compiler of this work, Umm Mujaahid Khadijah Bint-Lacina, was raised in a small town in the heartland of middle America. She graduated with honors from the University of Wisconsin only a short time after embracing Islaam and starting to live her life as a committed Muslim. She has been blessed with eight Muslim children she is committed to raising, and is regularly involved in various endeavors to benefit herself, fulfill the responsibility to her household, as well as her community and this blessed Ummah. Additionally, she has, in the years before traveling overseas to seek knowledge of this religion, previously run two successful small business enterprises from home - despite her main occupation as a Muslim mother and wife.

By Allaah's mercy she has been studying Islaam and the Arabic language generally since the time she embraced Islaam almost twenty years ago, and both of these subjects intensively for the past nine years from scholars and students of knowledge in the various centers of learning in Yemen and through the books and recorded lectures of the scholars of the Sunnah from throughout the world. Related to her studies in Arabic, she successfully completed two independent study seminars from the Islamic University of Medina while in the United States before having been blessed with the opportunity to study in Yemen. After beginning her language studies in Yemen with the well-known University of Medina Arabic language series through a private tutor, she then built upon this with the study of related classical works of Arabic Grammar when she started studying at Dar Al-Hadeeth in Mab'ar as well as other recommended works with a focus on works related to the fundamental beliefs of Islaam.

She later was blessed to continue her studies of this deen for three years in Dar Al-Hadeeth in Damaaj where she benefited from several excellent teachers. Among them was her daily class with Umm Salamah, may Allaah preserve her, previously the wife of Sheikh Muqbil, with whom in daily study she completed the work Bulugh al-Maram with the exception of two individual chapters due to illness. There she also benefited from the weekly class of the daughter of Sheikh Muqbil, Umm 'Abdullah, and from the lectures of well-known scholars of Ahlis Sunnah throughout Yemen who would come to address the students at the center. She has always striven to benefit from the people of knowledge in every city where her family resided in Yemen, while always making her home the center of her efforts to both study and teach this perfect religion.

May Allaah forgive us, her, and all the Muslims their errors and shortcomings, and guide us to every matter of belief, statement, and action that pleases Him alone.

Compilers Introduction (Pocket Edition)

All praise is due to Allaah Alone. We praise Him, seek His help, and ask His forgiveness. We seek refuge in Allaah from the evil of our souls, and the adverse consequences of our deeds. Whomsoever Allaah guides, there is none who can misguide him, and whoever He misguides, there is none who can guide him.

I bear witness that there is nothing worthy of worship except for Allaah; He is alone and has no partners. I bear witness and testify that Muhammad, may Allaah's praise and salutations be upon him and his family, is His perfect worshipper, and messenger.

Oh you who believe! Fear Allaah, as He deserves, and die not except as Muslims. -(Surat al-'Imraan, Ayat 102)

Oh mankind! Fear your Lord, Who created you from a single soul, and from him, He created his wife, and from these two, He created multitudes of men and women. Fear Allaah, from Whom you demand your mutual rights, and do not cut off the ties of kinship. Verily, Allaah is Ever-Watcher over you. -(Surat an-Nisaa', Ayat 1)

Oh you who believe! Fear Allaah, and say righteous speech. He will direct you to do righteous deeds, and He will forgive you your sins. And whoever obeys Allaah and His Messenger has indeed achieved the ultimate success. -(Surat al-Ahzaab, Ayat 70-71)

As to what follows: then the best of speech is the speech of Allaah, and the best guidance is the guidance of Muhammad, may Allaah's praise and salutations be upon him and his family. And the worst of affairs are newly invented matters (in the religion), and every newly invented matter is a misguidance, and every misguidance is in the Hellfire.

To Proceed:

Alhamdulillah, the position of the woman in Islaam is undoubtedly one of honor. The woman who is strong in her religion and who follows the teachings of the Qur'aan and Sunnah is respected and a great trust and responsibility is laid upon her shoulders. She is the one who is primarily responsible for raising and educating her children with an Islamic education. She is responsible for their physical health as well as their emotional and spiritual well-being. She is responsible for the organization and running of her household- and this includes budgeting, decorating, planning and preparing meals, caring for sick children, serving her husband and being his companion and helper, and so much more. While it is not forbidden that the woman work outside the home, her primary role in life is found within the comfort and security of her own home, as we shall see in the pages that follow- and this is a very great position, and a most elevated role, as we will see as we read the words of the scholars on the pages that follow, insh'Allaah. Concerning this, Sheikh Saalih al-Fauzaan, may Allaah preserve him, says, The third appendix was taken from an article in *"al-Asaalah"* magazine. In it the author lists several suggestions, based upon evidences from the Qur'aan and Sunnah, which, if we implement them in our family lives, our lives will become happier and richer, by the Grace and Mercy of Allaah. I chose to include this, as it is a very simplified listing, which brings everything down to clear and basic suggestions in a form that is easy to refer to and understand, insh'Allaah. Listed here are suggestions for BOTH the husband and the wife, Alhamdulillah, to take note of and try to implement, insh'Allaah.

I have tried, in this work, to define all of the Arabic words clearly the first time that they are mentioned, and then to use the transliteration of the word subsequently in order for the reader to become familiar with certain important Arabic terms. Most Arabic terms are italicized, with the exception of some that are common and understood by the majority of Muslims, insh'Allaah. In many instances I put in the original Arabic word for those who can read the Arabic, as transliteration is an inexact science at best, and the Arabic is best for proper pronunciation and better comprehension. I have done my best to transliterate each word clearly and precisely, and to be consistent in these transliterations. For Qur'aan, I relied mostly upon "*The Noble Qur'aan: English Translation of the Meanings and Commentary*", translated by Dr. Taqi ad-Din al-Hilali and Dr. Muhammad Muhsin Khan, may Allaah reward them. Concerning sources of *ahaadeeth*, I have in general relied on the scholars presenting them concerning their authenticity, though in many cases I had to additional research, as their sources were not always listed in the original work or transcription. Abu Sukhailah assisted me in this, may Allaah reward him for his efforts. To the best of our knowledge, all those quoted herein are people of good standing, and Allaah knows best.

Lastly, I would like to thank Umm Usaama, Sukhailah Bint Khalil, for all of her work assisting me in the publication of this book, from transcribing and translating two of the selections, to editing, and to holding the baby while I typed one last paragraph here or there. Also, Abu Hamzah, Hudhaifah ibn Khalil, who assisted in finding pertinent rulings and in research and translation for some of the rulings. I would like to thank, as always, Abu Sukhailah for his assistance, encouragement, support and technical and religious knowledge- he has been beneficial in the production of this book every step of the way. Also, my deepest gratitude and love goes out to those scholars who are guiding lights to the rest of us, who assist us and encourage us to live Islaam, and to be firm and strong in our religion. May Allaah preserve those who are amongst us today such as Sheikh Saalih al-Fauzaan, and Sheikh Rabee'a ibn Haadee al-Madkhalee, Sheikh Muhammad al-Imaam, and may he have mercy upon those who have passed, such as Sheikh 'Abdul-'Aziz Ibn Baaz, Sheikh Muhammad ibn Saalih al-'Utheimeen, Sheikh Al-Albani, and Sheikh Muqbil.

I ask that Allaah correct my mistakes, preserve my intentions, and accept this work from me, and I pray that the Muslim *ummah* in general, and my Muslim sisters specifically, benefit through it. Any good in this work is from Allaah alone, who has no partners, and any evil is from myself and the accursed *Shaytaan*. All praise is for Allaah alone, through whom all good deeds are completed.

Umm Mujaahid
Khadijah Bint Lacina
al-Amreekiyyah as-Salafiyyah

Related Islamic Rulings from the Major Scholars

Compiled & Translated by

Umm Mujaahid

Rulings Regarding

Aqeedah

(Beliefs)

The Conditions of Islaam

*Q*uestion: What are the conditions of Islaam?

*A*nswer from Sheikh 'Abdul 'Aziz ibn Baaz, may Allaah have mercy upon him: The conditions of Islaam are two:

The First Condition: Sincerity of intention for Allaah alone (الإخلاص , *al-ikhlaas*); and that you desire by your Islaam and entering into the religion of Allaah and by your actions, the face of Allaah, Glorified and Exalted is He. There is no doubt but that this is from it. This is because every action that is performed and it is not done seeking the face Allaah- whether it be the prayer, charity, fasting, or other than these- there is no benefit in it, and it is not accepted. This includes *ash-shahadatain* (testifying that there is no god worthy of worship except Allaah, and that Muhammad is His Messenger) if it is done to impress the people or hypocritically; it is not accepted and it will not benefit you, and you will be of the hypocrites.

It is necessary that your saying, "I testify that there is no god worthy of worship except Allaah, and I testify that Muhammad is the Messenger of Allaah in truth, and that he is the Messenger of Allaah sent to the *thaqaleen* (i.e. both the *jinn* and mankind), and he is the seal and last of the prophets"- if that is said by you truthfully, and with sincerity of intention for Allaah alone, then it will benefit you. Likewise, you are worshipping Allaah alone through your prayer, as well as in your charity, recitation, your saying "*La ilaha ila Allaah*", your fasting, and your pilgrimage- these are all for Allaah alone. (and the compiler of "*at-Tuhfat al-Baaziyyah*" adds a note here, as proof of this statement, the statement of Allaah, the Most High, ❧ *Say, "Verily, my prayer, my sacrifice, my living, and my dying are for Allaah, the Lord of the 'aalameen (mankind, jinn and all that exists).*❧- (Surat al-An'aam, Ayat 162)

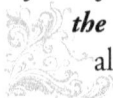

The Second Condition: Conformance to the Islamic legislation. It is necessary that your actions conform to the Islamic legislation, and are not from your opinion or your independent reasoning. Rather, it is necessary that you study and seek information concerning what conforms with the Islamic legislation, so that you pray as Allaah has legislated, fast as Allaah has legislated, give the obligatory charity as Allaah has legislated, make *jihaad* as Allaah has legislated, make the pilgrimage as Allaah has legislated it- so everything is approached like this.

The Prophet, may Allaah's praise and salutations be upon him, said, *{One who performs a deed which is not in conformance to that which we have been sent with, it is rejected.}* (This hadeeth is authentic, and is found in al-Bukhaari 2/116, Muslim 2/25,4/437, Abu Daawud 4606, Ibn Maajah 14, ad-Daaraqutanee pages 52 and 521, Ahmad 6/`46, 180,240,256, and 270 and other than them)

Allaah says in His Noble Book, *◊Or have they partners (with Allaah – false gods) who have instituted for them a religion which Allaah has not ordained?◊*- (Surat ash-Shooraa, From Ayat 21) Allaah, Glorified is He, reproaches them for this action.

And He, Glorified is He, says, "*Then We have put you (Oh Muhammad) on a (plain) way of (Our) commandment [like the one which We commanded Our Messengers before you. So follow you that (Islamic monotheism and its laws), and follow not the desires of those who know not. Verily, they can avail you nothing against Allaah (if He wants to punish you).◊*- (Surat al-Jaathiyah, From Ayats 18-19)

So it is obligatory to follow the Islamic legislation, which Allaah has legislated through the hand of His Messenger, Muhammad, may Allaah's praise and salutations be upon him, and to avoid leaving it in all of the acts of worship through which one becomes close to Allaah, Glorified is He, Most High.

These are the conditions of Islaam, and they are two conditions: The first is purity of intention for Allaah in action (including belief, speech and the action of the limbs) and the second is conformance to the Islamic legislation. This is that which will bring you benefit in your acts of worship, and through which Allaah will accept your worship from you, if you are Muslim.

("at-Tuhfat al-Baaziyyah fee al-Fataawa an-Nisaa'iyyah" Pages 56-57; originally from Fataawa min Noor 'ala ad-Darb)

The Fundamental Beliefs in Regard to Creed

Question: **What are the fundamental beliefs of ahl-as-sunnah wa ahl-al-jama'ah' concerning matters of creed and other matters related to the religion?**

Answer from Sheikh Muhammad ibn Saalih al-'Utheimeen, may Allaah have mercy upon him: The fundamental principle of *ahl-as-sunnah wa ahl-al-jama'ah'* in regard to creed and other matters related to the religion is complete adherence to the Book of Allaah and the Sunnah of His Messenger, may Allaah's praise and salutations be upon him, as well as the guidance and Sunnah which the righteous *khalifas* (Abu Bakr, 'Umar, 'Uthmaan, and 'Ali, may Allaah be pleased with all of them) followed, in accordance with the words of Allaah, the Most High,

❴*Say (Oh Muhammad): "If you (really) love Allaah, then follow me (i.e. accept Islamic monotheism, follow the Qur'aan and the Sunnah), Allaah will love you..."*❵– (Surat aal-'Imraan, From Ayat 31) Also, the statement of Allaah, the Most High,

❴*He who obeys the Messenger (Muhammad), has indeed obeyed Allaah, but he who turns away, then We have not sent you (Oh Muhammad) as a watcher over them.*❵– (Surat an-Nisaa', Ayat 80)

And the saying of Him, the Most High, ❁*And whatsoever the Messenger (Muhammad) gives you, take it; and whatsoever he forbids you, abstain (from it).*❁ – (Surat al-Hashr, From Ayat 7)

And though this chapter was revealed regarding the distribution of the spoils of war, it is even more fitting in matters pertaining to the Islamic legislation. The Prophet, may Allaah's praise and salutations be upon him, used to address the people on the day of *Jumu'ah*, saying,

{To proceed: Truly, the best speech is the Book of Allaah, and the best guidance is the guidance of Muhammad, may Allaah's praise and salutations be upon him. And the worst of matters (in the religion) are the newly invented matters, for indeed every newly invented matter is an innovation, and every innovation is a misguidance, and every misguidance is in the Fire.} (Muslim, 867)

And the Prophet, may Allaah's praise and salutations be upon him said, *{Adhere to my Sunnah and the Sunnah of the rightly guided khalifahs who came after me. Hold firm to it and cling to it with your molar teeth. And beware of newly invented matters, for indeed every newly invented matter is an innovation, and every innovation is misguidance.}* (Abu Daawud, 4607)

The proofs of this are many; so the way of *ahl-as-sunnah wa ahl-al-jama'ah* and their methodology is complete, in compliance with the Book of Allaah, the Sunnah of His Messenger, may Allaah's praise and salutations be upon him, and the Sunnah of the rightly guided *khalifahs* who followed him. In this way they established the religion, and they did not differ in it, in obedience to the words of Allaah, the Most High,

❁*He (Allaah) has ordained for you the same religion (Islamic Monotheism) which He ordained for Nuh, and that which We have revealed to you (Oh Muhammad), and that which We ordained for Ibraaheem, Moosa and 'Eesa saying you should establish religion (i.e. to do what it orders you*

21

to do practically) and make no divisions in it (religion) (i.e. various sects in religion).– (Surat ash-Shura, From Ayat 13)

Even though differences did occur between them in matters in which it is permissible to utilize *ijtihaad* (utilizing independent judgment by the scholars, based upon the established texts), this differing did not then lead to a differing in their hearts. Instead, one finds that there was mutual affection and love between them in spite of this differing which did occur between them due to this *ijtihaad*.

("Fataawa Arkan al-Islaam", Vol. 1, No. 3)

How to Increase Faith

*Q*uestion: How can a person increase his faith, putting into effect the commands of Allaah, and fearing His punishment?

Answer from the Permanent Committee of Scholars in Saudi Arabia: That comes about by reading the Book of Allaah, and studying it, and contemplating its meanings as well as its rulings. Also, by studying the Sunnah of the Prophet, may Allaah's praise and salutations be upon him, and understanding the details of legislation which come from it, and the actions which are required by that. One must conform to the correct Islamic beliefs, both in action and speech, be mindful of Allaah, and the heart must take heed of His magnificence. He must remember the Last Day, and that which it contains of the reckoning, of rewards and punishments, of severity and that which will cause terror. Also he must take as companions those who are known to be righteous, and must shun and turn away the people of evil and wrongdoing.

("Qatf al-Azhaar al-Mutanaathara min Fataawa al-Mar'at al-Muslimah", Page 67)

Extremism and Negligence

*Q*uestion: What are the limits that, if mankind exceeds them in the religion, they are considered extremism (غلو *ghuloo*), and what is the definition of al-ghuloo? Likewise, what are the limits of negligence (التفريط *at-tafreet*) in regards to the religion?

*A*nswer from the Permanent Committee of Scholars in Saudi Arabia: The boundary in the religion which, if it is exceeded it is considered extremism, is to surpass or go beyond that which has been legislated.

الغلو: it is entering too deeply into a matter, going beyond its proper limits or being excessive concerning it. The Prophet, may Allaah's praise and salutations be upon him, prohibited excessiveness, when he, may Allaah's praise and salutations be upon him, said, *{Beware of extremism in the religion, as verily people which came before you were destroyed through extremism in the religion.}* (Ahmad and other than him, and its chain of narration is authentic; see *"as-Silsilat as-Saheehah"* of Sheikh al-Albaani, may Allaah have mercy upon him, No. 1283)

As for negligence (التفريط *at-tafreet*), then it is falling short in establishing that which Allaah has made obligatory, performing some acts of wrongdoing, such as fornication, backbiting, or carrying tales, as well as leaving off some of the other obligatory acts, such as respect for the parents, keeping the ties of kinship, returning the Islamic greeting and that which is similar to these. And with Allaah is the success, and may Allaah's praise and salutations be upon our Prophet, Muhammad, his family, and his companions.

What will the Women have in Paradise?

*Q*uestion: It has been stated that the men will have al-hoor al-'ain (beautiful maidens) in Jennah (Paradise). What will there be for the women?

*A*nswer from Sheikh Muhammad ibn Saalih al-'Utheimeen, may Allaah have mercy upon him: Allaah, Glorified is He, the Most High, states, regarding the blessings of Paradise:

◆*Therein you shall have (all) that your inner selves desire, and therein you shall have (all) for which you ask. "An entertainment from (Allaah), the Oft-Forgiving, Most Merciful."*◆– (Surat al-Fussilat, From Ayats 31-32)

And He, the Most High, says, ◆*...(there will be) therein all that inner selves could desire, and all that eyes could delight in and you will abide therein forever.*◆– (Surat az-Zukhruf, From Ayat 71)

It is well known that marriage is one of the things which the souls desire most, and so it will be found in Paradise for the people of Paradise, whether they be men or women. So Allaah, Glorified is He, the Most High, will marry the woman in Paradise to the man who was her husband in the life of this world, as He, Glorified is He, the Most High, says,

"◆*Our Lord! And make them enter the 'Adn (Eden) Paradise (everlasting Gardens) which you have promised them – and to the righteous among their fathers, their wives, and their offspring! Verily, You are the All-Mighty, the All-Wise."*◆– (Surat Ghafir, Ayat 8)

If she did not marry in the life of this world, then Allaah, the Most High, will marry her to one whom she is pleased with in Paradise.

("Fataawa Arkaan al-Islaam" Vol. 1, No. 58)

The Majority of the People of the Hellfire

*Q*uestion: Is it true, as has been said, that most of the people of the Hellfire will be women, and why?

Answer from Sheikh Muhammad ibn Saalih al-'Utheimeen, may Allaah have mercy upon him: This is true, as the Prophet, may Allaah's praise and salutations be upon him, said, while delivering a speech to them, *{Oh gathering of women! Give charity, as I have seen that you are the majority of the people of the Hellfire.}* This doubt raised by the questioner was expressed to the Prophet, may Allaah's praise and salutations be upon him, as they said, "For what reason, oh Messenger of Allaah?" He, may Allaah's praise and salutations be upon him, replied, *{You curse frequently and are ungrateful to your husbands.}* (Agreed upon)

Thus, the Prophet, may Allaah's praise and salutations be upon him, made clear the reasons why they are the majority of the inhabitants of the Hellfire; because they malign, curse, and revile others frequently, and they are ungrateful to their husbands. Due to these reasons, they are the majority of the people of the Hellfire. ("*Fataawa Arkaan al-Islaam*" Vol. 1, No. 59)

Associating with the Disbelievers

*Q*uestion: What is the ruling concerning visiting the disbelievers, accepting gifts from them, attending their funerals, and wishing them well on their holidays?

Answer from Sheikh Saalih al-Fauzaan, may Allaah preserve him: There is no problem with visiting the disbelievers for the purpose of calling them to Islaam. As the Prophet, may Allaah's praise and salutations be upon him, visited his uncle Abu Taalib, and was present there, and he called him to Islaam (see "*Saheeh al-Bukhaari*", 2/98, from

the hadeeth of Sa'eed ibn al-Museeb, on his father).
He also visited the Jews, and called them to Islaam (see
"*Saheeh al-Bukhaari*",2/97, from the hadeeth of Anas
ibn Maalik). As for visiting the disbelievers just for pleasure
or comfort, then this is not permissible, because that which is
obligatory is hatred of them and separating from them.

It is permissible to accept gifts from them, because the Prophet,
may Allaah's praise and salutations be upon him, accepted
gifts from some of the disbelievers- for example the gift of
al-Maqooqs, the king of Egypt (see "*Nasb ar-Raayah*" 4/421,
"*Zaad al-Ma'aad*" 3/691-692)

It is not permissible to congratulate them on their holidays,
because that is showing attachment and support of them, and
acceptance of their wrongdoing. ("*al-Muntaqa min Fadeelatu
ash-Sheikh Saalih al-Fauzaan*" 1/255, as quoted in "*Fataawaal-
'Aqeedah*" of Sheikh Saalih al-Fauzaan, Page 31)

Review and Discussion Questions

Questions for 'Aqeedah rulings

Review:

1. What are the conditions of Islaam, as stated by Sheikh Bin Baaz, may Allaah have mercy upon him? (pages 18-19)

2. List some of the proofs that we must adhere to the Qur'aan and the Sunnah as understood and practiced by the salaf as-saalih. (page 21)

3. Define ghuloo and tafreet, and give an example of each in the religion. (page 23)

Discussion & Consideration:

4. If you ask almost any Muslim if he follows the Qur'aan and the Sunnah, he will say, "Yes." What is the difference between this and that which ahl-as-sunnah wa ahl-al-jama'ah believe in regards to creed and religious matters?

5. What would you say to a person who said to you, "The men in Islaam get beautiful women in Paradise- what do the women get?"

6. How do we deal with the disbelievers in regards to visiting them and congratulation them on their holidays?

Rulings Regarding the Role of Women in Islaam

The Exalted Position of the Woman in Islaam

Question: Some of the people say that the women are deficient in intellect, religion, inheritance, and giving testimony. And some say, "Allaah has made them equal (to the men) in reward and punishment." What is your opinion? Are they deficient in regards to the legislation of Muhammad, or not?

Answer from the Permanent Committee of Scholars in Saudi Arabia, may Allaah preserve them all: The Islamic legislation has come with honor and respect for the woman, raising her status, putting her in the position for which she is best suited, safeguarding her and preserving her honor and dignity. As it is made obligatory upon the one who is responsible for her or her husband to spend upon her, to support her monetarily and otherwise in a good way, to take charge of her affairs, and to treat her well. Allaah, the Most High, says,

❴ *...and live with them honorably...*❵– (Surat an-Nisaa, From Ayat 19)

And it is verified that the Prophet, may Allaah's praise and salutations be upon him, said, *{The best of you are those who are best to your family, and I am the best to my family.}* (Authentic, see "*as-Silsalat as-Saheehah*")

Islaam has given the woman everything which is fitting for her from rights and Islamically legislated freedoms. Allaah, the Most High, says,

❴*And they (women) have rights (over their husbands as regards living expenses) similar (to those of their husbands) over them (as regards obedience and respect) to what is reasonable, but men have a degree (of responsibility) over them. And Allaah is All-Mighty, All-Wise.*❵– (Surat al-Baqara, From Ayat 228) And this includes all the various types of deeds and actions, such as buying, selling, rectification, responsibility, loans, trusts, and other than these.

And it has been made obligatory upon her that which is fitting for her, from acts of worship in obligatory matters. These are like those of the men in regard to purification, prayer, obligatory charity, fasting, pilgrimage, and that which is like them from the Islamically legislated acts of worship.

However, the ruling of the Islamic legislation concerning inheritance is that the woman gets half of that which the man receives, as she is not responsible for providing for herself or spending upon her house and children- as indeed the one who is responsible for that is the man.

Just as it falls to the man to be the one charged with care of the guests, the overall decision making and determination of affairs, preserving the wealth, and that which is similar to that.

Just as the testimony of two women is equivalent to the testimony of only one man in some circumstances. This is because the woman is prone to forgetfulness more often (than the man) due to that which is related to the way in which she is fashioned, from that which befalls her due to her menses, pregnancy, childbirth, and raising the children; her mind is busy with all of these things and may cause her to forget.

Concerning this, the evidences of the Islamic legislation are proof that her sister supports her testimony, as that adds to her own accuracy, and strengthens her performance of the act. And there are other matters which are specific to the women, in which the testimony of one woman is sufficient, such as matters of nursing, marital problems and that which is similar.

The woman is equal to the man in regards to the recompense, and rewards for faith, righteous action, and with pleasure in the good life of this world, as well as the great rewards of the life of the Hereafter. Allaah, the Most High, says,

◆ *Whoever works righteousness – whether male or female – while he (or she) is a true believer verily, to him We will give a good life (in this world with respect, contentment and lawful provision), and We shall pay them certainly a reward in proportion to the best of what they used to do (i.e. Paradise in the Hereafter).* ◆ – (Surat an-Nahl, Ayat 97)

Along with that, it is known that the woman has rights, and that also upon her are obligations, just as the man has rights and obligations. There are matters for which the men are suited, which Allaah has entrusted to the men, just as there are matters for which the woman is suited which Allaah has entrusted to the women. And with Allaah is the success, and may His praise and salutations be upon our Prophet, Muhammad, his family, and his companions. ("*Qatf al-Azhaar al-MutanaQathara min al-Fatawaa al-Mar'at al-Muslimah*", Volume 1, Page 21-22)

Explanation of the Woman being Deficient in Intellect and Religion

*Q*uestion: *We always hear the noble hadeeth which states that the women are deficient in intellect and religion. Some of the men take from this that they can oppress or abuse the women. We would like for you to clarify the meaning of this hadeeth.*

Answer from Sheikh 'Abdul 'Aziz Bin Baaz, may Allaah have mercy upon him: It is clear that the hadeeth of the Messenger of Allaah, may Allaah's praise and salutations be upon him, is that he said, *{I have not seen one who is deficient in intellect and religion more able to affect the intellect of a reasonable man than one of you women.}* So it was said to him, "Oh Messenger of Allaah, what is deficient in her intellect? He, may Allaah's praise and salutations be upon him, said, *{Is it not true that the testimony of two women is equal to that of one man?}* It was then said, "What is deficient in her religion?" He replied, *{Is it not the case that the one who is on her menses does not pray, nor does she fast?}* (Authentic, found in al-Bukhaari, 3/384, Muslim, 2/694, 695, 1000, and other than them, in both this form and shortened form)

So he, may Allaah's and salutations be upon him, clarified that her deficiency in intellect is due to her weakness in recollection, and so her testimony is to be supported by another woman; and that is to give accuracy to her testimony due to the reasons that she may forget, or add something in her testimony.

As for the deficiency in her religion, then it is in the case of the menses and post childbirth bleeding, when she leaves off praying, and does not fast, and she does not perform the prayers; so this is from her being deficient in the religion. However, there is no blame upon her for this deficiency, and this deficiency is a result of Allaah's legislation, Glorified and Exalted is He. He, Glorified is He, Most High, is the One who has legislated it as a mercy for her, and to make things easy for her. As if she fasts when she has her menses and the post childbirth bleeding, she is harmed by that- so from the Mercy of Allaah is that He has legislated for her that she leave the fast. As for the prayer, due to her having her menses there issues forth from her that which negates the purification- so from Allaah's mercy, Glorified and Exalted is He, is that He legislated that she temporarily leave off the prayer. This is also the case during the post childbirth bleeding; then He has legislated for her that she not perform the prayer because there is great hardship in performing it due to its being repeated five times in the day and the night. And the menses can be for many days, as it may continue for seven or eight days, and the post childbirth bleeding for forty days. So it is from Allaah's mercy upon her, and His benevolence, that He has removed from her the prayer, both its obligation and performance (i.e. it is not obligatory for her to make up the missed prayers).

And this does not make it necessary that her intellect is considered deficient in every area, or that her religion is deficient in every matter. As indeed, the Messenger, may Allaah's praise and salutations be upon him, explained that the deficiency in her intellect was in the aspect of that which occurs from a lack of accuracy, and the deficiency in her religion is from the aspect of what occurs from the leaving of the prayer and fasting when she is on her menses or post childbirth bleeding. Yet one should not necessarily conclude from this that she is lesser than the man in everything, and that the man is better than her in everything.

Yes, the form of the men is better than the form of the women in general, due to many reasons, as Allaah, Glorifed is He, and Most High, as Allaah says,

Men are the protectors and maintainers of women, because Allaah has made one of them to excel the other, and because they spend (to support them) from their means.- (Surat an-Nisaa, From Ayat 34)

However, she may be raised above him in some instances in many matters- as how many of the women are superior to many of the men in intellect, religion, and reliability? And this is along with it being related from the Prophet, may Allaah's praise and salutations be upon him, that the form of the women is inferior to the form of the men in intellect and religion from these two aspects which he has explained.

She may put forth many righteous acts, which raise her above many of the men, due to those righteous acts and her fear of Allaah, Glorified and Exalted is He, as well as in her position in the Hereafter. She may have consideration in some of the matters in which she has significant reliability, and so she is more reliable than some of the men concerning them. And this is in many matters in which she works, and strives hard in her memorization and accuracy. So she could be an expert in Islamic history, or in many other matters. This is clear to anyone who examines closely the state of the women in the time of the Prophet, may Allaah's praise and salutations be upon him, as well as after that. By this it is known that this deficiency does not prevent relying upon her in narration, and likewise in testimony if it is supported by another woman, and it also does not prevent her having fear of Allaah, and being from among the best from among both the male worshippers of Allaah and the female worshippers of Allaah if she stands firm upon her religion. And this is despite her not having to fast during the time of her menses or post childbirth bleeding- being relieved of its immediate performance, but not its general obligation (meaning, she is responsible for making it up at a later date), and with her not having to pray, being relieved of both its performance and its obligation.

Therefore this does not require that she be deficient in everything, from the aspect of fear of Allaah, or from the aspect of her establishing His commands, or from the aspect of her reliability in that which she is an expert from other knowledge based areas. As it is a specific deficiency in the intellect and religion, as the Prophet, may Allaah's praise and salutations be upon him, made clear.

So it is not proper that a Believer accuse her of being deficient in everything, and weak in her religion in every matter. As indeed it is a specific weakness in her religion, and a specific weakness in her intellect, due to what is connected to the weakness of the testimony and such as is related to that. It is necessary that one be just and fair to her, and take the Prophet's, may Allaah's praise and salutations be upon him, words upon the best and most perfect of meanings. And Allaah knows best. ("*Fataawa al-Mar'at*" Pages 189-191, "*Majmoo' al-Fataawa wa Maqaalaat Mutanawa*" 4/292-294, as quoted in, "*at-Tuhfat al-Baaziyyah fee al-Fataawa an-Nisaaiyyah*", Volume 3, Pages 152-154)

General Advice to the Righteous Muslimah

*Q*uestion: Is there a comprehensive statement of advice for that Muslim woman whose priority has become a preoccupation with running around to different stores, thereby falling short in many obligations due to her persistence in that behavior?

*A*nswer from Sheikh Saalih ibn Fauzaan ibn 'Abdullah al-Fauzaan, may Allaah preserve him: A comprehensive statement of advice directed toward the Muslim woman is that she fear Allaah concerning herself, her husband and her children. So she must perform her household duties, raise and educate her children, and fulfill the rights of her husband. She must learn the affairs of her religion and be diligent in performing those things which Allaah has made obligatory. She should also perform many of recommended acts and give a good deal of charity, as much as these matters are within her capabilities. She should not leave her house except out of necessity, and when she does go out she must be completely covered (with the Islamically legislated *hijaab*), without perfume or beautification while she is out. She must also avoid riding alone with a driver who is not *mahram* for her.

She must not crowd together with the men outside or unnecessarily mix with them, or go to the male doctor alone, without a *mahram* with her. Likewise she must not travel without a *mahram*. She should seek medical care from female doctors, and not from the male doctors, except under these two conditions:

The First: There is no female doctor to be found

The Second: It must be necessary for her to go to him in order to be cured

The Muslim woman should stay far away from resembling the men or the female disbelievers in her hairstyle, clothing, and methods of beautification. She should hasten to marry if she is not married, and should not remain without a husband, and should be willing to abandon some of her other goals when she finds a righteous husband.

Concerning this, it is upon the Muslim woman to not pay heed to those senseless callers who desire to strip the woman of her honor and chastity, as they call her to leave the bounds of the legislated behavior of Islaam and to disobey the one who is in charge of her affairs who looks after her well-being.

Similarly, it is upon her to be dutiful to her parents, and to keep the ties of kinship, and to respect her neighbors and to refrain from doing them harm. And Allaah is the One who grants success, and may His praise and salutations be upon our Prophet, Muhammad, and upon his family and Companions. ("*Naseehah wa Fataawa Khaasat bil-Mara'at al-Muslimah*", a collection of rulings and advices from Sheikh Fauzaan, Pages 29-30)

Concerning Calling to Allaah

Question: Is it the domain of the woman to call to Islaam outside of her house, and how so?

Answer from the Permanent Committee of Scholars in Saudi Arabia, may Allaah preserve them: The place for women to call to Islaam first is in home, to her family, including her husband, the women, and those men who are *mahram* to her (those whom she is permanently forbidden to marry). And there is for her a place in Islamic *da'wah* outside of her home as well, addressing the women- as long as this does not include travelling without her husband or a *mahram*, and there is no fear of *fitnah*. And this must be with the permission of her husband if she is married, and she is motivated to do this through its necessity- and this must not cause her to leave off of that which is a greater obligation upon her from the rights of her family. And success is from Allah, and may His praise and salutations be upon our Messenger, Muhammad, his family, and his Companions. ("*Fataawa al-Lejnatu ad-Daa'ima*" 12/249, as quoted in "*Qatf al-Azhaar al-Mutanaathirah min Fataawa al-Mar'at al-Muslimah*" Page 860)

Question: How should we call the general people to as-salafiyyah (adhering the to Book of Allaah, and the Sunnah of His Messenger, may Allaah's praise and salutations be upon him, according to the understanding and practice of the Pious Predecessors), the way of the Pious Predecessors-especially since the people have a strong attachment to those who only invite to evil and wickedness?

Answer from Sheikh Rabee'a al-Madkhalee, may Allaah preserve him: Allah has made clear to us the correct manner of calling to Him. Allaah says to His Prophet,

❨*Invite (mankind, Oh Muhammad) to the way of your Lord with wisdom (i.e. with the Divine Revelation and the Qur'aan) and fair preaching, and argue with them in a way that is better.*❩- (Surat an-Nahl, From Ayat 125)

Calling to Allaah with wisdom- and wisdom is knowledge, clarification and establishment of the proof. So call with knowledge, good manners, kindness and gentleness- and this is in regards to the common person as well as those who are not common people. However, most of those who will receive the message are general people, who may accept the truth without arguing or disputing. And if it is necessary to resort to argument or debate, such as if someone has within him something from stubbornness, or something from adhering to deviation, then argue with him with that which is best. Allaah, the Most High, says,

❨The good deed and the evil deed cannot be equal. Repel (the evil) with one which is better (i.e. Allaah orders the faithful believers to be patient at the time of anger, and to excuse those who treat them badly) then verily he, between whom and you there was enmity, (will become) as though he was a close friend. But none is granted it (the above quality) except those who are patient – and none is granted it except the owner of the great portion (of happiness in the Hereafter, i.e., Paradise, and of a high moral character) in this world.❩– (Surat al-Fussilat, Ayats 34-35)

As someone does not possess such wisdom, except that he is the owner of the something tremendous. (From *"at-Tahdheer min ash-Shar"* as quoted in, *"Qatf al-Azhaar al-Mutanaathirah min Fataawa al-Mar'at al-Muslimah"* Page 67)

Review and Discussion Questions

Questions for Rulings concerning the Role of women in Islaam

Review:

1. List two proofs (one verse and one hadeeth) showing that the man must treat his wife well. (page 29)

2. What conditions does Sheikh Fauzaan, may Allaah preserve him, list for the person to go to a doctor of the opposite sex? (page 36)

3. Is it permissible for a woman to give da'wah outside her home? If so, what conditions must be met before she does so? (page 37)

Discussion & Consideration:

4. What are some matters in which the women and the men are equal in Islamic legislation? What are some matters in which they differ?

5. In the light of Sheikh Bin Baaz's, may Allaah have mercy upon him, explanation of the hadeeth of the woman being deficient in her intellect and her religion, what would you say to one who said to you, "Islaam says that women are stupid and weak"?

6. How should we begin calling the general people to Islaam?

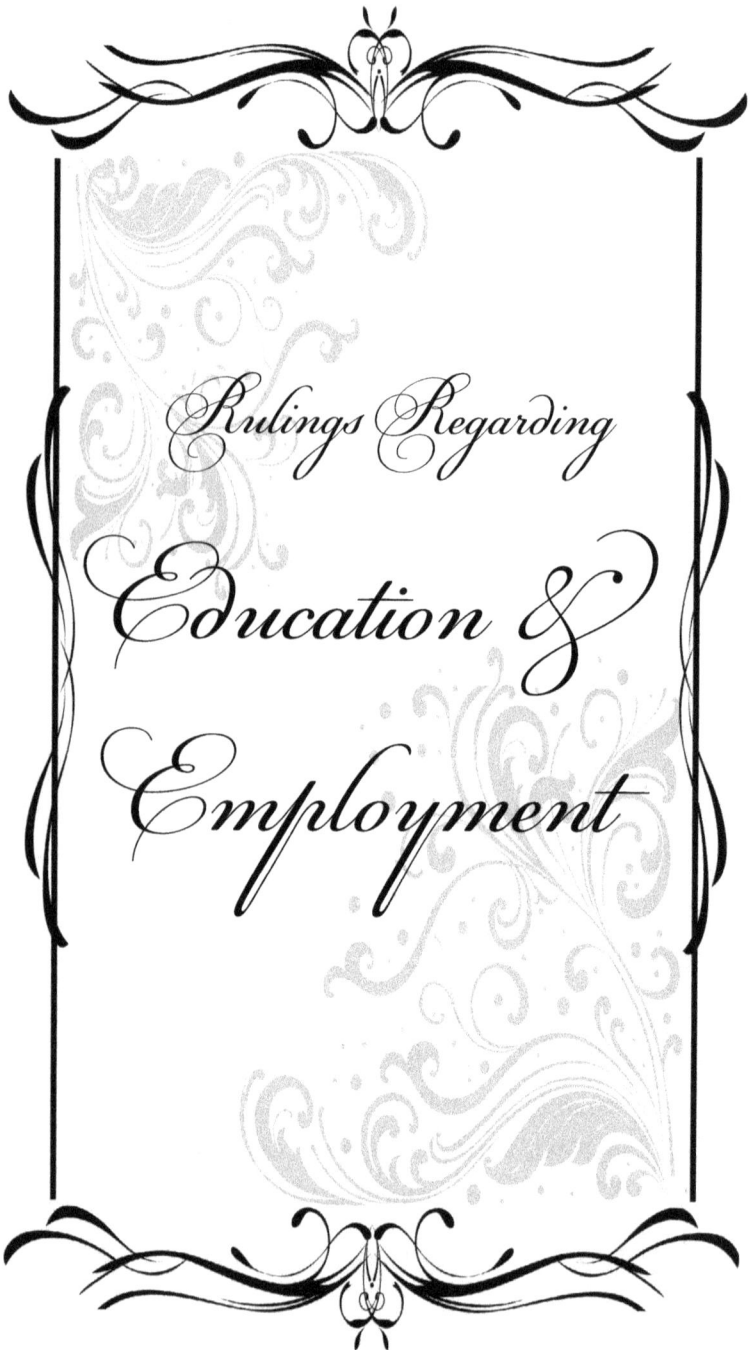

Rulings Regarding

Education &

Employment

The Muslim Woman Attending Islamic Lectures or Going to the Masjid

*Q*uestion: Is it allowed for the Muslim woman to go to the masaajid and Islamic lectures?

*A*nswer by Sheikh Saalih Fauzaan, may Allaah preserve him: Yes, it is definitely allowed for the Muslim women to go to the *masaajid* and Islamic lectures, as long as they are screened by being behind the men; as the Prophet, may Allaah's praise and salutations be upon him, said, in the hadeeth of Ibn Masood, *{Put them back where Allaah put them back.}* (Saheeh Ibn Khuzaymah 1596, Musannaf Abdu-Razzaq 4960, Al-Mu'jam Al-Kabeer 9330) And he said in the hadeeth of Abu Hurairah, *{The best of the men's rows is the first and the worst of them is the last, and the best of the women's rows is the last and the worst of them is the first.}* (Muslim 693, Ibn Khuzaymah 1469, Saheeh Ibn Hibban 403, Abu Daawud 586, Ibn Maajah 996, At-Tirmidhi 213) So if they go to the *masaajid* and attend Islamic lectures then this is a good thing.

And the caller to Islaam should give the women a separate lecture, as the Prophet, may Allaah's praise and salutations be upon him, gave them a separate lecture specific to them.

In Saheeh Al- Bukhaari Jaabir bin Abdullah narrated, *{The Prophet, may Allaah's praise and salutations be upon him, stood up on the day of Eid and started with the prayer ,and after that he delivered the khutbah (for the men). When the Prophet of Allaah, may Allaah's praise and salutations be upon him, had finished he went to the women and preached to them.}* And this is a proof that the women need a *khutbah* specifically for themselves.

The problem can be solved if a curtain is set up between the women and the men, so that they can hear the teacher's words and can send up questions, and the teacher can answer their questions with a divider and screen being present. ("*Naseehah wa Fatawaa Khaasat bi al-Mar'at al-Muslimah*" Page 42-43)

41

Advice to Women, to Remain in their Homes, to Pray, Study and Recite within Them

In the name of Allaah, the Most Gracious, the Most Merciful

Assalaamu Aleikum wa Rahmatullaahi wa Barakatuhu

Sheikh Saalih al-Fauzaan, may Allaah preserve him, was asked, "Esteemed Sheikh, may Allaah guide you and grant you success, this questioner from Libya asks, 'What is the ruling of the group reading for the women in the *masjid* for the purpose of learning and reviewing; and if it is not permitted, do the women leave the *masjid* for this matter?"

He, may Allaah have mercy upon him, answered, saying,

By Allaah, there is no doubt that the women staying in their houses- whether for prayer, or learning Qur'aan- their being in their houses- there is no doubt that this is the foundation. And if they make it a habit to go out to learn Qur'aan, and I do not know what else they undertake- then this distances them from remaining in the houses.

So it is my opinion that the women studying in the houses, and their prayer in their houses- this is the foundation, and it is the best for safeguarding her.

Now it is the case that the women get up and leave their houses in cars, and they are those who go out. And women love and desire this getting up and leaving and going out. Yet you men opened up this possibility now. It has become the case that they are not accustomed to the houses, and they do not establish the household. And they make the excuse that they are studying and I don't know what else.

So it is my opinion that the best thing is to abandon it, and that the women stay in the houses, and the knowledge they have is enough, insh'Allaah; there is no need to delve beyond necessity into outside places of education...yes.

This transcribed from a voice recording. From the website *Sahaab as-Salafiyyah*

Reconciling Bbetween Seeking Knowledge and the Family in Regard to Time

Question: How does a person reconcile between seeking knowledge and the family in regard to time- which of them is most important concerning that?

Answer from Sheikh Saalih Aal ash-Sheikh, may Allaah, the Most High, preserve him: There is no doubt that that which is obligatory is given preference over that which is superogatory. Some of the knowledge is obligatory; that which rectifies and perfects your belief is a personal obligation upon every Muslim. And it is those answers to the three questions- the three fundamental principles- Who is your Lord? What is your religion? Who is your prophet? Learn that, with its evidences- this is a personal obligation upon every Muslim, it is necessary that he learn it, even if he neglects some of the rights of the family in order to do so.

Likewise, if he is ignorant of *fiqh*, the intended guidance of the source texts, his worship will not be correct, and his prayer will not be correct. If he is a person with wealth, how does he give charity and what is its proper place, and other than that. It is obligatory that he learn these things.

So if the knowledge is obligatory, then it is given priority over that which is superogatory. If the knowledge is not obligatory, and there are obligatory matters which are in opposition to the non-obligatory matters, then the obligatory matter is given preference. For example, the right of his parents, or the right of his family and his wife and children- as he cannot neglect this obligatory right over him for the purpose of accomplishing a superogatory matter from the acknowledged superogatory matters.

The people differ in their situations; from them are those who are busy, and from them are those whose family relies upon him, and from them are the ones who are only moderately relied upon- they differ. And that which is obligatory is that the person puts the obligatory matters first, and the superogatory matters after the obligatory ones.

And you cannot get closer to Allaah, Glorified and Exalted is He, by anything which is more beloved to Him, than that which Allaah, Glorified and most High, has enjoined upon him, as comes forth in the authentic hadeeth, *{My slave does not draw near to me with anything dearer to me than that which I have enjoined upon him, and my slave continues to draw near to me through those acts which are preferred but not obligatory until I love him.}* (Bukhaare 6147, Ibn Hibaan 348) Meaning, after those things which are obligatory.

So it is necessary- from deeds- to give precedence to the obligatory matters over the superogatory matters. The Prophet, may Allaah's praise and salutations be upon him, said, *{Indeed your family has rights over you, and your soul has rights over you, and your Lord has rights over you. So give to each one who has rights upon you, his right.}* (Narrated with this wording on Ibn Masood in Hilyat al-Awliyaa 14877, and authentically on the Prophet with similar meaning in Sunan Abu Dawood 1175, and Sunan at-Tirmidhe 2395)The obligatory matters are many, so perform that which is obligatory, and the obligatory matters are given preference over the superogatory matters, and the application of that is not understood except with the practice- and give priority to the legislated obligatory matters over personal pleasure.

The farthest away from that is that some of the people

go to the superogatory acts, and not to the obligatory ones. Or rather, focus on that which is permissible, but neither rewarded nor punished (*mubaahaat*)- while neglecting the obligatory matters. He stays up all night engaging in various activities, and he leaves his family, and in this way he leaves the obligatory matters whose performance is demanded of him. His father may be elderly, and it would be difficult for him to take care of the household affairs, and the son goes off to gossip, "he said and he said", or does whatever he wants- and by his actions he is neither performing an obligatory nor a superogatory act- and in addition to that, he also neglects that which is obligatory..

There is no doubt that many of the people's problems and their opposition to that which is legislated - many of the problems and complaints which occur from the family concerning the children, and the fathers concerning the children, and from the wife concerning the husband, and the husband concerning the wife- they are from the failure to perform the obligatory duties, and failure to give priority to the obligatory matters over those which are recommended but not obligatory, and to give priority to these over those acts which are merely permissible, but are not rewarded or punished.

The true system which Allaah sent His Prophet, may Allaah's praise and salutations be upon him, with is proceeding in the call from the foundational principle. And the firm pillar is only worshipping Allaah alone, free from and devoid of the murky blemish and flaw of associating others with Allaah, and innovating in the religion, and wrongdoing. And any call which is built upon other than this foundation, then it is destined to rapid failure and there is no place of acceptance for it. (From the tape, "*Qawaa'id al-Qawaa'id*", the fifth question on the first side)

Becoming Firm in Knowledge

*Q*uestion: I desire to seek knowledge in my house through reading the books of Islamic jurisprudence and memorizing some of the ahaadeeth- however, I quickly forget that which I have memorized. How can I become firm in the knowledge I have?

*A*nswer from Sheikh Muqbil ibn Haadee al-Wadi'ee, **may Allaah have mercy upon him**: That which I advise every male and female Muslim with is to stay far away from any blameworthy actions and wrongdoing and to fear Allaah, Glorified and Most High. As blameworthy actions and wrongdoing weaken the understanding, and cause that which is memorized to leave. Likewise, also Allaah has said in His Noble Book,

❨*Oh you who believe! If you obey and fear Allaah, He will grant you furqaan [(a criterion to judge between right and wrong)*❩ – (Surat al-Anfaal, from Ayat 29)

As if we fear Allaah, Glorified and Most High, Allaah will bring light to our hearts, while wrongdoing darkens the heart, as is found in "*Saheeh Muslim*" from the hadeeth of Hudhaifah, may Allaah be pleased with him. in which the Messenger of Allaah, may Allaah's praise and salutations be upon him and his family, said, *{Turmoil and trials will be presented to the hearts as a reed mat is woven stick by stick, and any heart which accepts them will be marked with a black mark, while any heart which rejects them will have a white mark placed upon it. The result is that there will become two types of hearts: one like a white stone which will not be harmed by any turmoil or trial, as long as the heavens and the earth endure; and the other black and dust covered like an upset vessel, not recognizing that which is good, nor rejecting that which is hated, drinking in from that which is from its desires.}* (Muslim, 144)

Also, from *"Jaami' at-Tirmidhi"*, from Abi Hurairah, may Allaah be pleased with him, that the Prophet, may Allaah's praise and salutations be upon him and his family, said, *{When a worshipper of Allaah commits a sin, a black mark is made within his heart. If he repents, this is polished away, and if he commits a sin again (repeatedly), then a black mark is made within his heart, until the heart is covered by ar-raan.}* (at-Tirmidhi, 9/253, and it is found in *"al-Jaami"*, 6/232)

Meaning, it is eventually enveloped by the black marks of their sins. Then the Prophet, may Allaah's praise and salutations be upon him and his family, recited the saying of Allaah, the Most High,

Nay! But on their hearts is the raan (covering of sins and evil deeds) which they used to earn. – (Surat al-Mutafifeen, Ayat 14)

So it is necessary that we fear Allaah, Glorified is He, Most High Also, one must act according to any hadeeth (which one has memorized), as this will establish it more firmly in the mind, as will mentioning it amongst the sisters. As az-Zuhri sat with his paternal aunt, and said a hadeeth to her, and she said, "By Allaah, I do not know what was said." So he said, "Be quiet, oh foolish one, when I am relating my information."

So when you call your sister to you, you mention that which you have learned to her, or to your husband- you tell him about it- then, Allaah willing, it will become more firmly established, and then, also, you will be upon good- a good that is better than becoming busy with "he said, she said", or being occupied with means of amusement and pleasure.

I advise you to not be rushed, but rather to persist upon this seeking of knowledge and acting upon it, as you do not know but that by the permission of Allaah, the Most High, an abundant yield may be produced from that- and knowledge is light, and Allaah, Glorified is He, Most High, puts it into the heart of whom He desires to from His

worshippers. He, the Most High, says,

❝*Allaah burdens not a person beyond his scope.*❞- (Surat al-Baqara, From Ayat 286), and,

❝*Allaah puts no burden on any person beyond what He has given him.*❞- (Surat at-Talaaq, From Ayat 7)

So if you are not able to memorize a whole page, then memorize half a page- do not then attempt to memorize a full page or an entire sheet. If you are able to memorize a short hadeeth, then do not try to memorize a long hadeeth that takes up half a page or a whole page. That which is important to note is that memorization is a gift from Allaah, Glorified is He, Most High, and it is like a heavy load someone carries- there comes a person who is able to carry a heavy rock and lift it up to his head, while another person is not able to even lift it up off the ground. So as for yourself, do not be in a hurry, as you are upon that which is something good, may Allaah bless you. (From "*Asilat al-Hadeedah*", as found in "*Fataawa al-Mar'at al-Muslimah*", a collection of rulings and advices from Sheikh Muqbil, may Allaah have mercy upon him, Pages 67-68)

Review and Discussion Questions

Questions for Rulings regarding education and employment

Review:

1. Is it permissible for the woman to go out to the masaajid and attend Islamic lectures? Is it better for them to remain in their homes? Explain. (page 41)

2. Make a numbered list summarizing Sheikh Muqbil's, may Allaah have mercy upon him, advice for making our knowledge firm in our hearts and minds. (page 47-48)

Discussion & Consideration:

3. What are some ways that a woman can obtain beneficial Islamic knowledge within her own home? How can she spread that knowledge to others in a permissible way?

4. Sheikh Saalih aal-Sheikh, may Allaah preserve him, explains that it is necessary to put the obligatory matters before the superogatory matters. Give two examples of this.

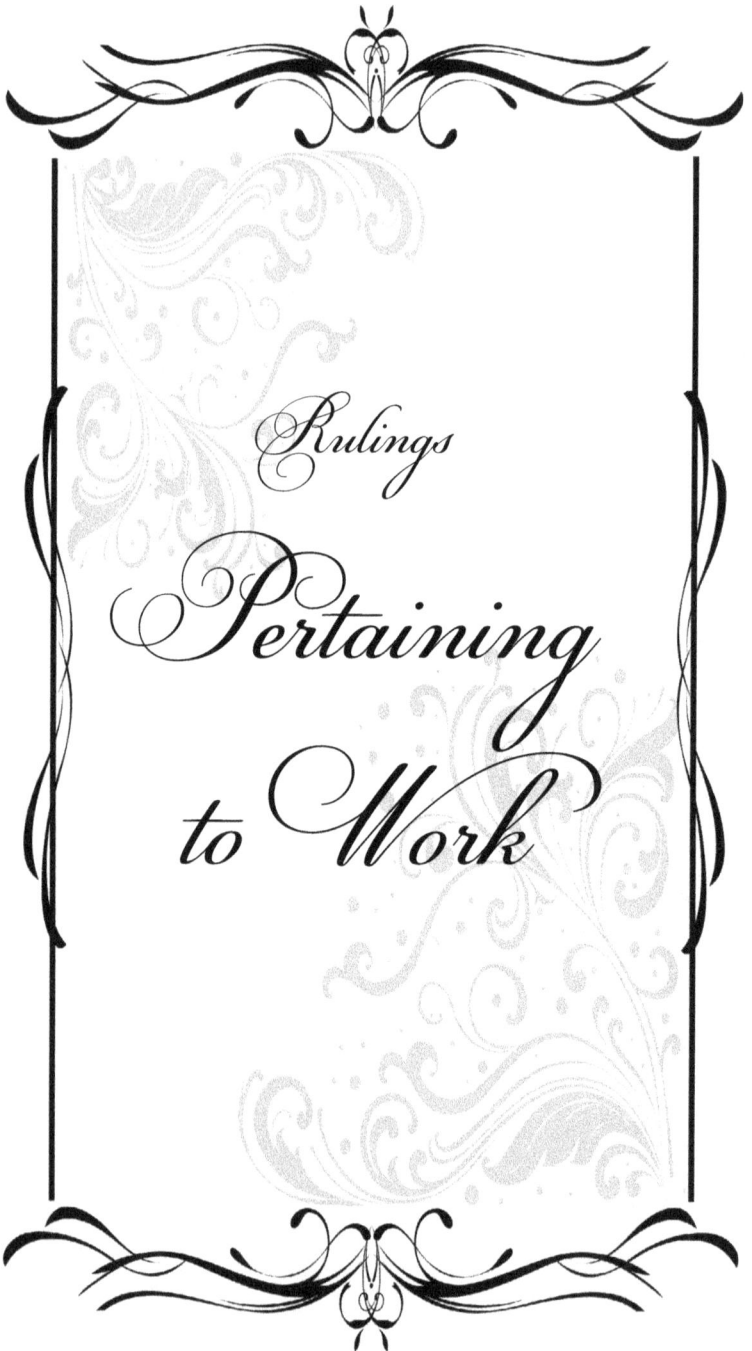

Rulings Pertaining to Work

*Q*uestion: *What is the ruling concerning the woman working when she is married?*

Answer from the Permanent Committee of Scholars in Saudi Arabia: It is not permissible for the woman to work in a situation in which there is mixing with the men, and this is regardless of whether she is married or unmarried. This is because Allaah, Glorified is He, created the men to incline toward and be attracted to the women, and He created the women to incline toward and be attracted to the men, along with there being present a weakness within them. As if there is mixing between the men and the women, then societal trials will occur, and it becomes a cause of corruption, because the soul is naturally inclined towards evil. However, it is permissible for her to work in a venue in which there is no mixing with the men, if she has the permission of her husband.

And Allaah grants all success, and may Allaah's praise and salutations be upon our prophet Muhammad, and his family and companions. ("*Fataawa al-Lajnatu ad-Daa'imah*" 17/234, as quoted in "*Qatf al-Azhaar al-Mutanaathirah min Fataawa al-Mar'at al-Muslimah*" Volume 2, Volume 2, Page 522)

*Q*uestion: *What is the ruling on the woman taking on jobs which it is possible for men to undertake instead of her, and this is done specifically - the creation of job openings intended for women?*

Answer From the Permanent Committee of Scholars in Saudi Arabia: The foundational principle in the Islamic legislation is for the woman to stay in her home which Allaah honored her with, and remain there, and stay away from the places of trials and questionable things, and not expose herself to harm, while taking care of her children's Islamic upbringing, and undertaking the serving of her husband and the matters of her household.

However, if she is forced to work then it is necessary for her to choose those jobs which are suitable for her religion and her worldly affairs, which will not interfere with taking care of her husband and children, if her husband consents to this. As for her competing with the men for the jobs which are in the men's field, then that is not permissible, because of the negative effects, harm, and evil which will come about because of that; for in giving her this opportunity there is the ruin of the men, and the suppression of the available opportunities for men's employment. Also her employment in these jobs exposes her to mixing with the men and temptations, and things will occur that will not have praiseworthy consequences. Added to that is the fact that this will interfere with her fulfillment of her obligations towards her husband, and the affairs of her household and children, which will make it necessary to pay others or hire servants, and that brings about more harm and causes problems in the upbringing of the children, as well as in the religion, as is not hidden from anyone.

And Allaah grants all success, and may Allaah's praise and salutations be upon our prophet Muhammad, and his family and companions. ("*Fataawa al-Lajnatu ad-Daa'imah lil Bohooth al-'Ilmiyyah wa al-Iftaa*" 18/236)

*Q*uestion: *Is it permissible for the husband to command his wife to work at a job if he is a person who is incapable of procuring the basic matters of living such as clothing and a place to live?*

*A*nswer from Sheikh al-Albaani, may Allaah have mercy upon him: It is not permissible. It is upon him to leave her in her house, and that he work in a job which will provide a living for them. As for causing her to leave his house to work in a workplace, and to mix with the men, then this is not permissible. ("*al-Haawee min al-Fatawaa* *ash-Sheikh al-Albaani"* Collected by Abu Yusuf Muhammad ibn Ibraaheem, Page 462)

*Q*uestion: *Afwaan; is it permissible for the husband to command the wife to work?*

*A*nswer from Sheikh al-Albaani, may Allaah have mercy upon him: If there is a legitimate excuse, then it is obligatory if it is a necessity; because it is obligatory upon the wife to obey her husband in that which he commands her with within the limits of the Islamic legislation. (*"al-Haawee min al-Fatawaa ash-Sheikh al-Albaani"* Collected by Abu Yusuf Muhammad ibn Ibraaheem, Page 462)

*Q*uestion: *If a woman works, with the permission of her husband, to whom belong the wages of her work?*

*A*nswer from Sheikh al-Albaani, may Allaah have mercy upon him: This differs; the affair differs per situation:

If a contract exists between the spouses, and the woman works and earns money through this work, and no condition has been made in the contract that the money is for her husband, or half is for her and half is for her husband, or this, or that, then the money remains with her. And the opposite is completely true if the contract does state this as a condition.

That which occurs today, wherein a man marries a woman, and she is, for example, a teacher and has a salary- then there may arise between them differing after that as to whom this salary of hers belongs.

We say, so long as the husband is content with the situation of the woman before he makes a contract with her, then it is not for him to share in her earnings or provisions. However, we have observed that her working takes from her time with her husband, as well as his comfort and her serving him in his house, as well as concerning the upbringing of children. So it is his prerogative to give her the option of staying in her work, and he shares in some of her wealth, or that she stay in her house and leaves her work. And I believe that there is no differing amongst the scholars that the husband, if he commands his wife with a command that does not differ from the Islamic legislation, then it is obligatory upon the woman to obey him, especially if it is due to the reason that she is so busy with her job that she falls short in managing the matters of her house and serving her husband. (From the audio series, "*Silsilat al-Hudaa wa an-Nur*", Tape Number 791, as quoted in, "*Qatf al-Azhaar al-Mutanaathirah min Fataawa al-Mar'at al-Muslimah*" Volume 2, Volume 2, Page 527)

Review and Discussion Questions

Questions for rulings pertaining to work

Review:

1. What reasons do the Permanent Committee of Scholars give for the impermissibility of the women working in jobs for which they compete with the men? (page 52)

Discussion & Consideration:

2. It is permissible for the woman to work outside of the home. Is this statement correct or incorrect? Explain your answer.

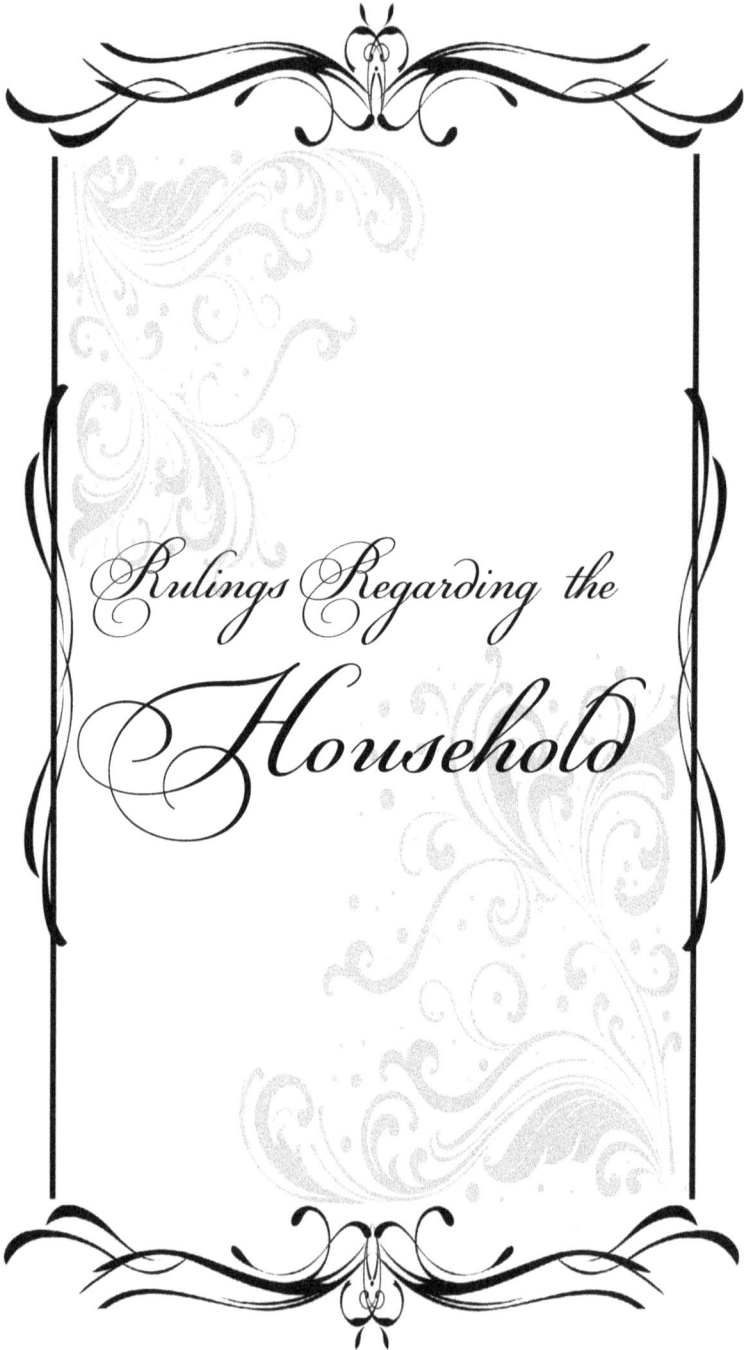

Rulings Regarding the Household

The Salafi House

*Q*uestion: What are the physical attributes which should be found in the Salafi house?

Answer from Sheikh al-Albaani, may Allaah have mercy upon him: It is not possible to restrict the answer; as this differs from one person to another. As it is sufficient for the illiterate man to have a cupboard to keep his food, for example, while the scholar will additionally need a cupboard or shelf in which to keep books in. So each case is relative, and every person is aware of that which is necessary for him, or is not necessary for him. For example, the prayer rug; is it something which must be present in the Salafi household? The answer is no- it is sufficient to have an ordinary rug, one that is not adorned or of exceptional quality. Even this rug differs from one place to another. In a cold country, the rug is necessary; indeed it needs to be made of wool (for warmth). As for the hot country, if one sits upon the ground, a large room rug is itself not necessary, let alone a prayer rug as well. So in relation to that, the case is relative, as it differs from place to place- for example an air conditioner is necessary in hot countries, to assist one in seeking knowledge, whereas in Syria there is no necessity for it, as a small fan will take care of the heat. So the case cannot be specified in regard to every person in every place. ("*al-Haawee min al-Fatawaa ash-Sheikh al-Albaani*" Collected by Abu Yusuf Muhammad ibn Ibraaheem, Pages 462-463)

Spending of Wealth

*Q*uestion: There is textual evidence that Allaah loves to see the sign of His blessings upon His worshipper; and some of the women spend a lot of money on their clothing and matters concerning beautification. What do you say in regard to this?

Answer from Sheikh Saalih ibn Fauzaan ibn 'Abdullah al-Fauzaan, may Allaah preserve him: The one whom Allaah blesses bestows permissible wealth, Allaah has blessed him with this favor, and it is obligatory upon him to be grateful for it. This is through giving charity with it, and purchasing food and clothing- but this is without extravagance or that which is doubtful. And the action of some of the women, spending extravagantly or excessively when purchasing clothing, or buying a lot of things without necessity, is only out of pride or a desire to show off and keep up with the latest fashions advertised- all of that is from the wastefulness and extravagance which is prohibited, and wasting money.

It is obligatory upon the Muslim woman to be moderate in regards to that, and to stay far away from *at-tabarruj* (going out dressed or beautified in an improper manner) and exaggeration concerning matters of beautification- especially when leaving the house.

Allaah, the Most High, says, *and do not display yourselves like that of the times of ignorance*- (Surat al-Ahzaab, From Ayat 33)

And He, the Most High, says, *And tell the believing women to lower their gaze (from looking at forbidden things), and protect their private parts (from illegal sexual acts) and not to show off their adornment except that which is apparent* to His, the Most High, saying, *And let them not stamp their feet so as to reveal what they hide of their adornment.*- (Surat an-Noor, From Ayat 31)

And we will be asked concerning this wealth on the Day of Judgment, as to where we acquired it, and how we spent it. ("*Naseehah wa Fatawaa Khaasat bil-Mara'at al-Muslimah*", a collection of rulings and advices from Sheikh Fauzaan, Page 71)

*Q*uestion: *If a Muslim woman makes a lot of different food, and makes it attractive in order to make her husband happy, is this from the vanity in the world and worldly things which we are responsible for from wealth and luxury?*

Answer from Sheikh Muqbil ibn Haadee al-Wadi'ee, may Allaah have mercy upon him: There is no problem with this, insh'Allaah- however *az-zuhd* (abstinence, simplicity) is better. Allaah, Glorified is He, and Most High, says, ◊*Oh Children of Adam! Take your adornment (by wearing your clean clothes) while praying [and going round the Ka'bah], and eat and drink but waste not by extravagance, certainly He (Allaah) likes not al-Musrifoon (those who waste by extravagance).*◊– (Surat al-A'raaf, Ayat 31)

So if there is anything left from the food, do not throw it away. Rather, it is necessary that it goes out to the poor and destitute. The matter is simple, insh'Allaah- it is not necessary to restrict or oppress ourselves, but *az-zuhd* is better, and the state upon which the Prophet, may Allaah's praise and salutations be upon him and his family, was upon is best. It has been narrated from 'Umar, may Allaah be pleased with him, and look at its truthfulness, *"Prepare yourself for a rough life, as indeed the blessings do not endure."* (Narrated by Ibn Abi Shaybah in *"Kitaab al-Aadaab"*, No. 80. Its chain of narrations is weak, however it has other narrations which support and strengthen it)

It is necessary that we prepare for rough times, and prepare for hunger, so that when the matter occurs we do not remain as though we are young chickens- it is necessary that we become accustomed to deprivation. And Allaah knows best. (*"Fataawa al-Mar'at al-Muslimah"* Pages 368-369. Originally found in "Questions from the Young Algerian Women")

Listening to the Qur'aan while Working in the House

*Q*uestion: *I spend a good portion of time- long hours- in the kitchen in order to prepare food for my husband. I wish to benefit from my time, so I listen to the Noble Qur'aan, either on the radio, or a recording. Is my action in this correct, or is it not proper for me to do this, as Allaah, the Most High, says, "So, when the Qur'aan is recited, listen to it, and be silent that you may receive mercy." - (Surat al-A'araaf, From Ayat 204)*

A nswer from Sheikh Saalih al-Fauzaan, may Allaah preserve him: There is no problem with listening to the Noble Qur'aan on the radio or from a recording while people are working, and there is no contradiction between this and His saying, "…listen to it, and be silent…" because the silence is required in accordance to that which is possible- so the one who is working is quiet and listens to the amount that he is able. ("*Fataawa al-Mar'at al-Muslimah*", a collection of rulings concerning women from various scholars, Page 578)

Review and Discussion Questions

Questions for Rulings regarding the household

Review:

1. What verse does Sheikh Muqbil bring concerning the encouragement to az-zuhd? (page 59)

Discussion & Consideration:

2. How can we find balance in our households between being miserly and spending extravagantly?

3. What are some possible examples of how we can fulfill our obligations to the household but still benefit in a secondary way at the same time?

Rulings Regarding

Marriage

Regarding Living with the Wives Honorably

*Q*uestion: *Some of the young men, may Allaah guide them, are generally concerned with adhering to the religion, yet they do not live with their wives honorably, as they busy themselves working a great deal, or spending their time studying and working- but they leave their wives alone or with their children in the house for long periods of time, due to their needing to work or study. What do you, Esteemed Sheikhs, say, concerning that, and are work and seeking of knowledge to be done at the expense of the time for the wife? Benefit me, and may Allaah benefit you.*

Answer from Sheikh 'Abdul 'Aziz ibn Baaz, may Allaah have **mercy upon him:** There is no doubt that it is obligatory upon the husbands to live with their wives in an honorable fashion, as Allaah, Glorified and Exalted, says,

❴*...and live with them honorably.*❵- (Surat an-Nisaa, From Ayat 19)

As well as His, Glorified is He, saying, ❴*And they (women) have rights (over their husbands as regards living expenses) similar (to those of their husbands) over them (as regards obedience and respect) to what is reasonable, but men have a degree (of responsibility) over them. And Allaah is All-Mighty, All-Wise.*❵- (Surat al-Baqara, From Ayat 228)

Also, the saying of the Prophet, may Allaah's praise and salutations be upon him, to 'Abdullah ibn 'Amr ibn al-'Aas, may Allaah be pleased with them both, to the one who busied himself with standing in the night prayer, and fasting during the day, ❴*Fast, and break the fast. Sleep, and stand in prayer. Fast from each month three days, as every good deed is worth ten like it. As you have a right upon yourself, and your wife has a right upon you, and your guest has a right upon you- so give to each one his rights.*❵ (Authentic, narrated in al-

Bukhaari, 1153,1976,1977,1978,1979,3418,3419,5 052, and Muslim 2/812, 1159, at-Tirmidhi, 3/550, Abu Daawud, 1/739, 2427, and others)

As well as other *ahaadeeth* which have been reported concerning this. So that which is legislated for the young men and other than them is that they live with their wives honorably, and to beautify this living, and if it is possible for them to do their research or some of their other jobs in their home, whenever it is possible, then that is best for the family and children. So in any case, it is legislated for the husband to set aside a time for his wife, in order to make her happy, and treat her well. Especially if she is alone in the house and does not have anyone else with her except her children, or she does not have anyone to spend time with. As he, may Allaah's praise and salutations be upon him, said, *{The best of you is the one who is best to his family, and I am the best of you to my family.}* (Authentic, narrated by at-Tirmidhi, 10/363, 3904, Ibn Hibaan, 9/484, 4177, and ad-Daaramee, 2/159 by way of Hishaam ibn 'Urwah from his father, from 'Aishah) And his, may Allaah's praise and salutations be upon him, saying, *{The believers who have the most perfect faith are those with excellent character, and the best of you are the ones who are best to their wives.}* (*Hasan*, from the hadeeth of Abi Hurairah, may Allaah be pleased with him)

It is legislated for the wife that she cooperate with her husband in that which he must perform from studying or work, and to be patient concerning that which occurs of the shortening of time with her which cannot be avoided, so that there comes about cooperation between them, thus acting upon the saying of Allaah, Glorified and Exalted,

Help you one another in al-birr and at-taqwa (virtue, righteousness and piety)– (Surat al-Ma'idah, From Ayat 2) as well as the generality of his (the Messenger of Allaah's) saying, may Allaah's praise and salutations be upon him, *{The one who is concerned with the needs of his brother,*

Allaah is concerned with his needs.} (Authentic) And his, may Allaah's praise and salutations be upon him, saying, *{And Allaah assists the worshipper, as the worshipper assists his brother.}* (Authentic) (From "*Fatawaa Islaamiyyah*", 3/213, 214, as quoted in "*at-Tuhfat al-Baaziyyah fee al-Fataawa an-Nisaaiyyah*", Volume 2, Pages 185-186)

*Q*uestion: What is the Islamic ruling in your opinion concerning the one who beats his wife and takes from her wealth, and does these with severity, and he treats her in an evil manner?

*A*nswer from Sheikh al-'Utheimeen, may Allaah have mercy upon him: This person who beats his wife, takes from her wealth, and treats her in an evil manner is a wrongdoer, disobedient to Allaah; as Allaah, the Most High, says,

◈*...and live with them honorably.*◈– (Surat an-Nisaa, From Ayat 19)

And His, the Most High, saying, ◈*And they (women) have rights (over their husbands as regards living expenses) similar (to those of their husbands) over them (as regards obedience and respect) to what is reasonable*◈– (Surat al-Baqara, From Ayat 229)

And it is not permissible for him to treat his wife in this evil manner and then to go and demand from her that she treat him in a good manner, as this is from the oppression or injustice which falls under His, the Most High, saying,

◈*Woe to al-mutaffifoon (those who give less in measure and weight). Those who, when they have to receive by measure from men, demand full measure, And when they have to give by measure or weight to (other) men, give less than due.*◈– (Surat al-Mutafiffeen, Ayats 1-3)

So every person who takes his full right from the people, then does not give the people their full right, then he is included under these noble verses.

And that which I advise this person, and those like him, with, is: To fear Allaah concerning the women, as the Prophet, may Allaah's praise and salutations be upon him, commanded in his *khutbah* at 'Arafaat the year of the Farewell Pilgrimage, when he said, *{Fear Allaah concerning the women, as you have taken them as a trust from Allaah and they have been made permissible for you by the Word of Allaah.}* (Muslim 2212, Ibn Maajah 3072, Ibn Hibaan 1473, Sunan Ad-Daaramee 1842)

And I say to him, and the likes of him: It is not possible for you to have a happy life until the spouses treat each other with justice, goodness, and overlooking that which offends and taking notice of and acknowledging that which is good.

The Prophet, may Allaah's praise and salutations be upon him, said, *{The believing man should not dislike a believing women, as if he dislikes one aspect of her character, there is another aspect which he will be pleased with.}* (Muslim 2750, Musnah Ahmad 8179) (Collected in "*al-Fataawa al-Qayyimah lil-Usrat al-Muslimah*" Collected by Sa'eed 'Abdul-Ghafaar 'Ali, Pages 105-106)

Rights and Obligations of the Wife

*Q*uestion: *What are the rights of the wife, and those things which are obligatory upon her?*

*A*nswer from Sheikh Muhammad ibn Saalih al-'Utheimeen, may Allaah have mercy upon him: The rights and obligations of the wife and those matters which are upon her, are not necessarily specifically itemized in the legislation. Rather, they also refer back to that which is customary among people, as Allaah, the Most High, says, ◈*...and live with them honorably*◈- (Surat an-Nisaa, From Ayat 19), and His saying, ◈*And they (women) have rights (over their husbands as regards living expenses) similar (to those* *of their husbands) over them (as regards obedience and respect) to what is reasonable* - (Surat al-Baqara, From Ayat 228)

So that which is held to be customary among people concerning rights, then that is obligatory, and that which is not held to be customary, then it is not obligatory, except for those things which differ from that which is clearly Islamically legislated. So if it is the custom of the people that the man not command his family to perform the prayer, or to beautify their characters, then this is a false, wrong custom and is considered null and void. As for when the custom of the people does not differ from the Islamic legislation, then Allaah has referred to this in the preceding verses.

It is obligatory upon the ones responsible for the household to fear Allaah concerning that which Allaah has made them responsible for- and this is from both the men and the women- and that they not neglect these things. As it occurs that the man may neglect his children, both the boys and the girls, as he does not ask about which ones are absent, or present, and he does not sit with them. And a month or two may go by and he does not spend time with his children or wife. This is a tremendous error. Indeed, we advise our brothers to gather together with the family and to not be isolated, and that lunch and dinner be eaten with the family together- however without the wife sitting with men who are not *mahram* for her, as this is from those things which occur among the people from the evil customs which differ from the Islamic legislation, that they men and women all gather together to eat, even if they are not *mahram* for one another. (*"Fataawa al-Mar'at al-Muslimah"*, a collection of rulings concerning women from various scholars, Page 279)

*Q*uestion: *I am a woman who obeys her husband and follows the commands of Allaah, but I cannot meet my husband with joy and a clear face, because he does not fulfill that which is obligatory for him in the matter of providing me with clothing, and I shunned and turned away from him in my bed- so is there any sin upon me?*

*A*nswer from Sheikh Saalih ibn Fauzaan ibn 'Abdullah al-Fauzaan, may Allaah preserve him: Allaah, Glorified and Most High, has made it obligatory to have good relations between the husband and the wife, and that both of them give to the other his or her rights, so that they bring benefit to the marriage. And it is upon the husband and wife to be patient concerning the shortcomings of the other spouse, and with problems in their relationship, and to fulfill their obligations, as this is from the reasons which bring about a lasting marriage, its working well together and the endurance of the marriage. So my advice to you is to be patient with your husband's shortcomings, and give your husband his rights. That way, by the grace of Allaah, your ending will, insh'Allaah, be good. And through giving him his rights, it may come about that he would be encouraged to give you your rights as well. ("*Naseehah wa Fatawaa Khaasat bil-Mara'at al-Muslimah*", a collection of rulings and advices from Sheikh Fauzaan, Page 57)

*Q*uestion: *A wife falls short in fulfilling her obligations to her husband, her children, and her house, and she wishes to have a servant. Should she get a servant?*

*A*nswer from Sheikh Muhammad ibn Saalih al-Utheimeen, may Allaah have mercy upon him: The matter of having a servant has become one of pride and vanity if one does not truly have a need for one. And much of what comes about due to that is only a great trial; for example adultery or fornication between the owner of the house or his teenage sons and the servant, and such as occurs from the men who are servants entering the house, and what occurs from trials to the women of the house. Due to that, it is required that you do not bring servants into the house except if there is an extreme need to do so, and the servant must have a *mahram* with her.

As for the woman who desires a servant due to having a lot of housework, then it is necessary that her husband say to her," I am going to marry another Muslim woman, to assist you in the housework!" Then this wife will cease to ask for this thing.

In reality, this beneficial remedy is of advantage to the man, as all that increases marriages is best, and marrying more than one wife, if the man is able to fulfill his obligations, is better than restricting it. And the Prophet, may Allaah's praise and salutations be upon him, said, *{Marry the ones who are loving and bear many children, as I hope my ummah will be expanded through you.}* (Collected by Ahmad, at-Tabaraanee, and Abi Daawud by meaning) If the people are afraid due to the matters which occur between the two wives, then we say to him: Bring in a third, as this eases the disputes between the first two, as has been seen. Concerning this, they say that the one with three has it easier than the one with two. And if disputes occur between the three, then bring in a fourth. ("*Fataawa al-Mar'at al-Muslimah*", a collection of rulings concerning women from various scholars, Page 278)

*Q*uestion: Is it permissible for the husband to take pleasure in the whole of his wife's body, front and back, including between her buttocks, while not entering her anus?

*A*nswer from the Permanent Committee of Scholars in Saudi Arabia, may Allaah preserve them all: It is permissible for the man to take pleasure with his wife from any aspect of her body, excluding only the anus, intercourse during her menses or post childbirth bleeding, during *ihraam* for *Hajj* or *Umrah* until they have totally completed the rites.

And Allaah grants all success, and may Allaah's praise and salutations be upon our prophet Muhammad, and his family and companions. ("*Fataawa al-Lajnatu ad-Daa'imah*" 19/251, as quoted in "*Qatf al-Azhaar al-Mutanaathirah min Fataawa al-Mar'at al-Muslimah*" Volume 2, Page 607)

Concerning the Woman Raising her Voice to her Husband

*Q*uestion: What is the ruling concerning the woman raising her voice to her husband during conversation or argument?

*A*nswer from the Permanent Committee of Scholars in Saudi Arabia, may Allaah preserve them all: That which is permissible is that the husband and wife speak to each other in a manner which brings about love and affection, and which strengthens the marriage bonds, and that they both avoid raising their voices to their companion, or speaking in a manner which is disliked. Allaah, Glorified and Exalted is He, says, ❨*...and live with them honorably...*❩– (Surat an-Nisaa'a, From Ayat 19) It is not proper for her to raise her voice to him, as Allaah, Glorified is He, says, "***And they (women) have rights (over their husbands as regards living expenses) similar (to*** *those of their husbands) over them (as regards obedience and respect) to what is reasonable, but men have a degree (of responsibility) over them.*- (Surat al-Baqara, From Ayat 228)

However, it is necessary that the husband remedy any problem with that which is most suitable, in order that the strong emotion not be further intensified. And with Allaah is the success, and may Allaah's praise be upon our Prophet, Muhammad, his family, and his companions, and Allaah's salutations. ("*Fataawa al-Lejnatu ad-Daa'imah*" 19/247 as found in the book, "*Qatf al-Azhaar al-Mutanaathirah min Fataawa al-Mar'at al-Muslimah*" Page 623)

Review and Discussion Questions

Questions regarding rulings regarding marriage

Review:

1. What evidences does Sheikh Bin Baaz, may Allaah have mercy upon him, cite as proof that men must live with their wives honorably?? (pages 63-64)

2. What are three things that Sheikh Fauzaan, may Allaah preserve him, recommends for a successful, lasting marriage? (page 68)

Discussion & Consideration:

3. After studying this section, list some of the proofs given that the husband and wife should do their best to give each other their rights, and support and encourage each other in their individual undertakings? List five ways you can implement this in your own married life.

4. What advice would you give to the woman who desires that her husband hire a servant?

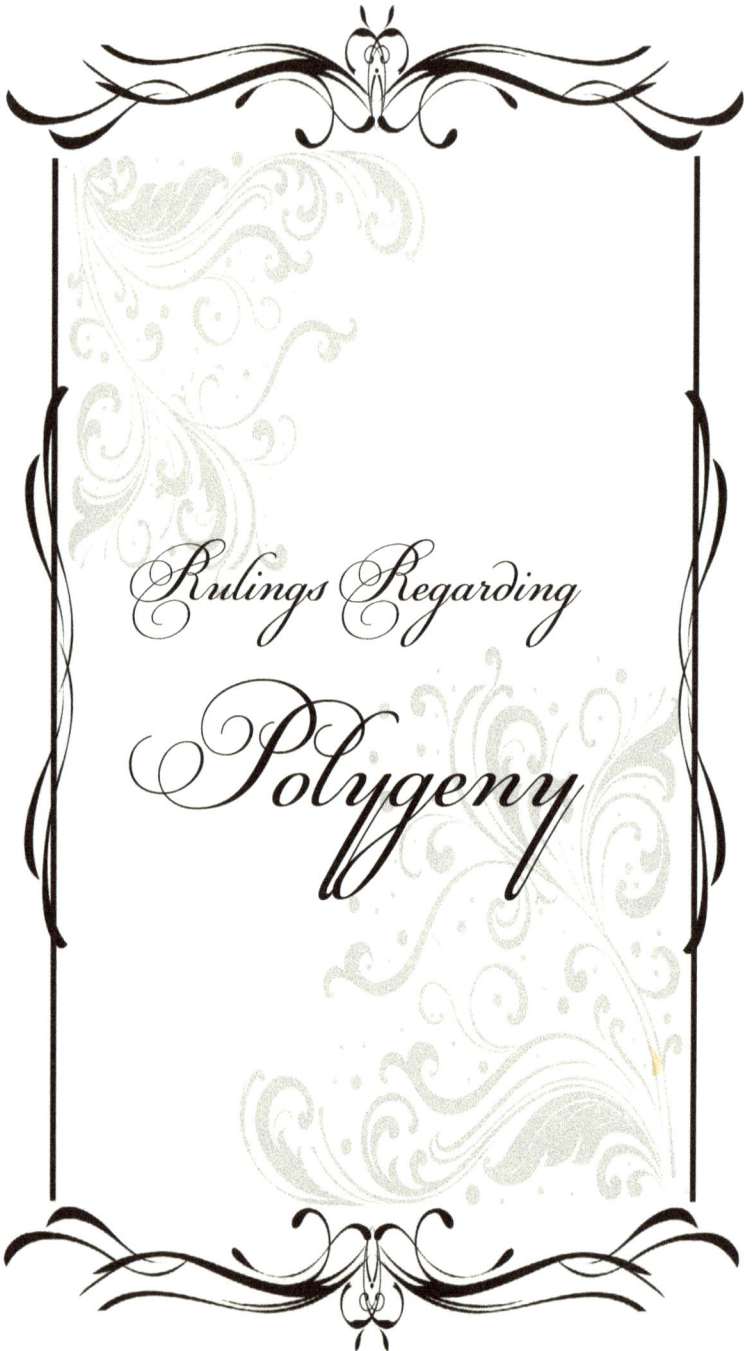

Rulings Regarding

Polygeny

*Q**uestion: A noble verse is mentioned in the Noble Qur'aan in regard to the place of polygeny (the practice of the man being permitted to marry up to four wives at one time) which says,*

❦*...but if you fear that you shall not be able to deal justly (with them), then only one...*❧- (Surat *an-Nisaa, From Ayat 3*)

And in another place, He, the Most High, says, "You will never be able to do perfect justice between wives even if it is your ardent desire❧- (Surat *an-Nisaa, From Ayat 129*)

So in the first, justice to the spouses if there is more than one is made a condition, while in the second it is made clear that the condition of justice is not possible to attain. Does this mean that the first verse is abrogated, and the marrying of more than one wife is not allowed because the condition of justice is impossible to achieve?

Answer from Sheikh 'Abdul 'Aziz ibn Baaz, may Allaah have mercy upon him: There is no contradiction between the two verses, nor is this a case wherein the first of the two is abrogated by the second. Indeed the justice which is commanded is that which is possible, and that is justice concerning the division of time and the giving of provisions. As for justice in love, the desire for intercourse, and such as these, then this is not possible. And this is what is meant in the saying of the Most High,

❦*You will never be able to do perfect justice between wives even if it is your ardent desire*❧- (Surat an-Nisaa, From Ayat 129)

Concerning this it has been established from the Prophet, may Allaah's praise and salutations be upon him, from the hadeeth of 'Aishah, may Allaah be pleased with her, in which she said, "The Messenger of Allaah, may Allaah's praise and salutations be upon him, divided between his wives and was fair, and he said, *{Oh Allaah, this is my division*

in that which I am capable; so do not blame me for
that which you are in possession of and which I do not
possess.} (Abu Daawud, at-Tirmidhi, an-Nasaa'ee, Ibn
Maajah, and Ibn Hibaan and al-Haakim have declared it to
be authentic. This hadeeth comes through various chains, and
is either *hasan* or *saheeh*, Allaah knows best) And with Allaah
is the Success. ("*Fataawa al-Mar'at*", Pages 108-109) as quoted
in "*at-Tuhfat al-Baaziyyah fee al-Fataawa an-Nisaa'iyyah*" Vol.
2, Page 228)

*Q*uestion: *A married man travelled from his country to*
another country, then married in the country in which
he was staying without the knowledge of his first wife. Is this
permissible according to the Islamic legislation?

*A*nswer from the Permanent Committee of Scholars in
Saudi Arabia, may Allaah preserve them: It is permissible
for him to marry a second wife without the permission of the
first- indeed, even without her knowledge, as long as he sees
a benefit in that, and he is able to support the wives and deal
justly between the two wives or all of the wives in that which
he is capable of, as Allaah, the Most High, says,

◊And if you fear that you shall not be able to deal justly with the
orphan girls then marry (other) women of your choice, two or
three, or four; but if you fear that you shall not be able to deal
justly (with them), then only one or (slaves) that your right hands
possess. That is nearer to prevent you from doing injustice.◊–
(Surat an-Nisaa', Ayat 3)

And from Allaah is the success, and may His praise and
salutations be upon our Prophet, his family, and his
Companions. ("*Fataawa al-Lejnatu ad-Daa'imah*", 19/79, as
quoted in "*Qatf al-Azhaar al-Mutanaathirah min Fataawa al-*
Mar'at al-Muslimah" Vol. 2, Page 634-635)

*Q*uestion: *Some of the women object to the matter of polygeny, or they object to their husbands entering into it- does this matter enter into some aspect of hypocrisy?*

Answer from Sheikh 'Abdul 'Aziz bin Baaz, may Allaah have mercy upon him: It is upon her to be content with the ruling of Allaah; however, her being pleased with having a companion co-wife- then this is not required. However, it is upon her to be content with the general ruling of Allaah concerning polygeny, and Allaah's wisdom is great and far-reaching. It is not permissible for her to dislike that or to deny it- but as regards to her being personally pleased, then some people cannot bear it; but it is upon her to listen to and obey her husband if she is able. And if she is not able due to circumstances, and she seeks a divorce, then this is due to her, and it is not required that her husband comply with her in this. However, if due to polygeny he sees from her that which he does not like, and that which is harmful, then it is better if he separates from her, as some of the women cannot endure this. ("*Fatawaa Kitaab ad-Da'wah*", 4/216, as quoted in "*at-Tuhfat al-Baaziyyah fee al-Fataawa an-Nisaa'iyyah*" Vol. 2, Page 229)

Review and Discussion Questions

Questions Regarding Rulings regarding Polygeny

Review:

1. What does the "justice" referred to in the verses concerning polygeny refer to? page 75)

2. Is it necessary that the first wife be informed that the husband is going to marry another? Explain. (page 77)

Discussion & Consideration:

3. If a woman dislikes that her husband marry a second wife, does this make her a hypocrite? Explain.

4. What practical advice can you come up with for yourself and others concerning dealing with the fact of polygeny? What are some things that might help to ensure that your marriage is a strong, successful one, and that you have retain a good relationship with your husband?

Rulings Regarding

Children

An Exhortation to have many Children

*Q*uestion: *A young man married and has three children, and he says, "My wife and I decided to prevent further pregnancies so that we may be able to raise our children with a correct Islamic upbringing, and to attempt to keep distant the many temptations that surround them. What is your opinion of this, may Allaah reward you?*

*A*nswer from Sheikh Muhammad ibn Saalih al-'Utheimeen, may Allaah have mercy upon him, said,

All praise is due to Allaah, Lord of the worlds, and I ask that His praise and salutations be upon our Prophet Muhammad, his family, his companions, and all those who follow them in righteousness until the Day of Judgment.

To Proceed:

This solution is not correct- I mean, the prevention of procreation, as this differs from that which the Prophet, may Allaah's praise and salutations be upon him and his family, guided to, since he said, *{Marry the ones who are loving and fruitful, as I desire to have the most followers from the prophets on the Day of Judgment.}* (Collected by Ahmad in his "*Musnad*" (13569) and at-Tabaraanee in ("*al-Awsat*", 5099, from the hadeeth of Anas, may Allaah be pleased with him, and Sheikh al-Albaani has declared it to be authentic due to a supporting hadeeth collected by Abi Daawud)

Because a person does not know if perhaps those children which he already has may die and he will be left with no progeny. The explanation that it (not having more children) is for the sake of having control over their upbringing and perhaps fulfilling the act of providing for them, is in reality an unsound justification. This is because righteousness is only by the Hand of Allaah, Glorified and Exalted is He. And education and upbringing is undoubtedly a cause as well- and how many of the people do not have but one child and fail in regards to his education and upbringing; and how many of the people have ten children and Allaah makes it possible to carry out their education and make them righteous by His Hand?

There is no doubt that the one who says, "If there are many children, it is not possible to control them"- this is having the bad suspicion of Allaah, Glorified and Exalted is He. And perhaps he will be punished for this suspicion. Rather, the steadfast believer performs those things which are legislated which are causes for success in undertaking education and upbringing and asks Allaah for assistance and success. And when Allaah knows from him that he is truthful and correct in his intention, Allaah will rectify his affairs for him.

So I say to the brother who asked the question: Do not do this- do not stop having children, do not stop having children. Have as many children as you are able, as their sustenance is upon Allaah, and their piety is upon Allaah. And the more you increase in educating and bringing them up, the more you will increase in reward. As if you have three and you teach them good character and educate and raise them well, you only have the reward for three. But if you have ten, then you are rewarded for ten- and you do not know if perhaps Allaah will make from those ten scholars and fighters in the way of Allaah who will benefit the Islamic *Ummah*, and that will be from the signs of your performance of good deeds. Have many children, and Allaah will increase your wealth, and make your provisions plentiful. (End of Sheikh al-'Utheimeen's exhortation)

(From "Fataawa Noor 'ala ad-Darb") as quoted in, "Tarbiyat al-Abnaa': Sawaal wa Jawaab", Pages 10-11)

Rulings Regarding Birth Control

Question: *What is the ruling on the woman taking birth control pills, or using an I.U.D or diaphragm (meaning, a barrier method of some sort) for contraception, particularly when it is a method which is specifically utilized by the woman?*

Answer from Sheikh Muqbil ibn Haadee al-Wadi'ee, may Allaah have mercy upon him: That which I advise you with is *al-'azl* (العزل) (this is what is known in the West as "withdrawal", wherein the man removes his private parts from inside the woman before ejaculation occurs), as this is what has been mentioned (in the Sunnah). As for the birth control pill, then in it there is harm, as well as blind following of the enemies of Islaam. From its harms is that it may cause inflammation or infection of the womb, which requires medical treatment- and this treatment may cure it, or it may not. Likewise the issue of using the barrier method- it, itself may break, or cause damage, or perhaps the sperm will come out, or it may cause irritation to the male organ, or the device may come out with the intimate relations. So that which I advise you with is the *al-'azl*, as it is that which has been mentioned and the Prophet, may Allaah's praise and salutations be upon him and his family, has permitted it.

("Fataawa al-Mar'at al-Muslimah", Pages 242-243)

*Q*uestion: *The questioner asks concerning the one who uses the birth control pill, or the injection, or al-'azl (withdrawal) to prevent contraception...*

*A*nswer from Sheikh Muqbil ibn Haadee al-Wadi'ee, may Allaah have mercy upon him:

As for the pill and the injection, then I do not know of them that they are established in the source texts. It is not proper to use them, because Allaah, Glorified is He, the Most High, says in His Noble Book, ❴*And kill not your children for fear of poverty.*❵ – (Surat al-Israa, from Ayat 31).

And the Prophet, may Allaah's praise and salutations be upon him and his family, said, *{Marry and have children, because I will compete with you against the other nations on the Day of Judgment.}* (Abu Daawud and other than him, from Ma'qil ibn Yasaar, may Allaah be pleased with him, and it has many supporting narrations and Sheikh al-Albaani has declared it authentic in "*as-Sunan*" and Sheikh Muqbil, may Allaah have mercy upon him, in his collection, "*Kitaab an-Nikaah*") And the Prophet, may Allaah's praise and salutations be upon him and his family, has informed man that Allaah will increase his wealth and children. (al-Bukhaari, 6378 and Muslim 268 and 141)

As for *al-'azl*, then it is permissible, and some of the people say that is permissible, but is disliked. It is permissible because Jaabir Ibn 'Abdullah, may Allaah be pleased with him, said, "*We practiced al-'azl during the period in which the Qur'aan was being revealed.*" (al-Bukhaari, 5208, and Muslim, 1440) And it has been reported that the Prophet, may Allaah's praise and salutations be upon him and his family, said when asked concerning *al-'azl*, *{It is the lesser burying alive.}* (Muslim, 141 from 'Aishah, may Allaah be pleased with her) And the Prophet, may Allaah's praise and salutations be upon him, said, *{There are none from the souls but that if Allaah decrees its creation, then it is created.}* (Muslim,

30-31) So using the withdrawal method of birth control is permissible. As for using the birth control pill or likewise the injection to prevent pregnancy, then this is not permissible due to that which is known regarding it. And this is that Allaah, Glorified is He, the Most High, said, *And kill not your children for fear of poverty.* – (Surat al-Israa, from Ayat 31). And in another verse, *kill not your children because of poverty* – (Surat al-An'aam, From Ayat 151)

So it is proper to know that Allaah, Glorified is He, the Most High, is more merciful to His worshippers than any person could be; He is the Most Merciful to the woman, and the Most Merciful to the child, and he is the Most Merciful to the married one; however, *al-'azl* is permitted.

("Fataawa al-Mar'at al-Muslimah" Pages 243-244)

Question: A woman has a small, ill child, and she is pregnant again. So she finds it difficult to care for her present children, and she finds the pregnancy difficult as well. Is it all right for her, after she gives birth this time, to use birth control pills?

Answer from Sheikh Muqbil ibn Haadee al-Wadi'ee, may Allaah have mercy upon him:

I advise her to entrust her affair with Allaah. And if she fears harm for herself, and if a Muslim doctor who is a specialist in this area has said that damage may come to her, and she may die due to pregnancy, then it is permissible for her to use that (the birth control pill).

("Fataawa al-Mar'at al-Muslimah", Page 245)

Regarding Naming of Children

Question: Allaah, Glorified is He, the Most High, has blessed me with a daughter, and I would like to give her one name, and my wife wants to name her something else. I proposed to her that we draw lots on paper with the two names, and name her according to the outcome of this drawing of lots- so is this from those things which are appropriate? And if it is not so, then how do we resolve this difference? And is the naming the right of the father, only? Benefit us, may Allaah give you good.

Answer from Sheikh 'Abdul 'Aziz ibn Baaz, may Allaah have mercy upon him: In this situation, drawing lots is from the accepted legislated matters, according to that which it contains for remedying the situation and pleasing the people involved. The Prophet, may Allaah's praise and salutations be upon him, used it in many matters, and it has been narrated from him that he, may Allaah's praise and salutations be upon him, drew lots between his wives when he had to travel, and the one whom the marked lot indicated went with him. (The hadeeth concerning this is found in al-Bukhaari, 2593, and Muslim, 8196). Also, when he advised the man to free some slaves, and he had six, and he did not have other than them, the Prophet, may Allaah's praise and salutations be upon him, drew lots between them, and he freed two, and kept four. (Muslim, 4425)

The naming of the child is from the rights of the father; however it is recommended that he consult the mother concerning this, in order to reconcile the two of them, and join their hearts. It is legislated for both of them that they choose good names, and avoid the disliked names. And it is not permissible to name them as the worshipper of other than Allaah, such as 'Abd an-Nabee (worshipper of the Prophet), 'Abd al-Ka'bah (worshipper of the Ka'bah), 'Abd al-Husayn, or similar to these. This is because all of worship is for Allaah, Glorified is He, and it is not permissible to worship other than Him.

And it has been related from the famous scholar Abu Muhammad ibn Hazm, that there is consensus among the scholars that this forbiddance of naming one as a worshipper of other than Allaah does not include 'Abd al-Mutalib, because the Prophet, may Allaah's praise and salutations be upon him, allowed this name for some of his companions, may Allaah be pleased with all of them. (He is 'Abd al-Mutalib, ibn Rabi'ah, ibn al-Haarith, ibn 'Abd al- Mutalib, ibn Haashim, al-Qursh al-Haashimee, and he is the son of the paternal uncle of the Prophet, may Allaah's praise and salutations be upon him.) And with Allaah is the success.

(From "Fatawaa Islaamiyyah lil-Musnad", 3/221, as found in the book, "Qatf al-Azhaar al-Mutanaathirah min Fataawa al-Mar'at al-Muslimah" Volume 2, Pages 491-492)

*Q*uestion: *Is it permissible to name my son Jibreel or Meekaa'eel? (These are the names of two of Allaah's angels)*

Answer from Sheikh Rabee'a al-Madkhalee, may Allaah preserve him: It is not forbidden- one is not forbidden from that. There is no prohibition concerning naming with the names of the companions, the generation after them, the scholars, and the prophets. As for naming with Jibreel, then there is no harm in that.

(From the tape called, "Inna Allaah la Yanza' al-Ilm Antazaa'an" as quoted in the book, "Qatf al-Azhaar al-Mutanaathirah min Fataawa al-Mar'at al-Muslimah" Volume 2, Page 494)

Nursing of Children

Question: Concerning the woman who "nurses" her child with formula, and not her own milk- is this considered nursing from the viewpoint of Islaam?

Answer from Sheikh al-Albaani, may Allaah have mercy upon him: Unquestionably, there are no texts upon this matter, so that it is from those matters whose answer must come from independent reasoning based upon evidence (الإجتهاد). That which is most apparent to me, and Allaah knows best, is that it is not considered nursing, because in the case of her "nursing" her child with the formula, then she does not exert herself and does not use her own body's nourishment as nourishment for her child. As for reserving all of her nourishment for herself, then this is like not nursing.

("al-Haawee min al-Fatawaa ash-Sheikh al-Albaani" Collected by Abu Yusuf Muhammad ibn Ibraaheem, Page 458)

Toys for Children and Teaching Children through the use of Pictures

Question: Here there are many types of dolls; from them are some that are made of cotton, and they are constructed of a sack or bag connected to a head, two hands and two legs. From them are some which resemble a human completely, and from them are those that talk or cry or walk. What is the ruling concerning making or buying the likes of these types for small girls in order to educate them and for their amusement?

Answer from Sheikh al-'Utheimeen, may Allaah have mercy upon him: As for those which are not found to be a complete or perfect image of a human being, in which there are limbs and a head but their resemblance to creation is not obvious or plain, then there is no doubt as to their permissibility, and that they are in the form of the dolls which 'Aishah, may Allaah be pleased with her, played with. As for those that completely resemble creation as though one were seeing a person, especially those which move or have a voice, then I find in myself that which causes me to dislike them and doubt their permissibility because they imitate Allaah's creation. That which is evident is that the dolls which 'Aishah, may Allaah be pleased with her, played with did not have these attributes and so it is best to avoid them. However, I do not place upon them the definite ruling of being forbidden, as the small children have that which is allowed to them, which is not allowed to adults in matters similar to this. As the children are naturally disposed to play and amusement and are not responsible for anything from the acts of worship, so that we say, "His time is wasted upon play and frivolity." And when the people desire to be cautious concerning this type of thing, then remove the head, or heat it so that it becomes soft, then squeeze or compress it until its features are removed.

("Majmoo' al-Fatawaa", 2/277, as quoted in "Qatf al-Azhaar al-Mutanaathirah min Fataawa al-Mar'at al-Muslimah", Pages 817-818)

*Q*uestion: *There are statements and rulings about children's toys which have become numerous. So what is the ruling concerning the dolls and animals and three dimensional toys with human form? There are some who have allowed keeping them with the condition that they are debased and that they are not given much importance; and there are some who have completely prohibited them. So what is the correct ruling? And what is the ruling of using the flash cards which have upon them pictures for teaching the children letters and numbers or the manner of performing wudhoo and salaat?*

*A*nswer from Sheikh Saalih al-Fauzaan, may Allaah preserve him: It is not correct to keep the pictures of things with souls except for necessary pictures like the pictures on the driver's license, that which is needed protect oneself, and the identity card. And pictures other than these are not allowed to be kept for children's toys or for teaching them because of the generality of the prohibition of picture making and their use. And there are many children's toys without pictures and there are other methods of teaching them without pictures. And whoever allowed the pictures for children's toys, then his saying is not sound because he is depending upon the hadeeth of 'Aishah the day when she was small. And it is said that the hadeeth of 'Aishah is abrogated by the narrations which prohibit the pictures. And it is said that the forms (dolls) were mentioned in it were not like the forms (dolls) of today. They were only made from pieces of cloth and sticks as was known in their time; they did not resemble animals in the same way as those toy animals which are known now. And this latter statement is the most correct saying. And Allaah knows best. And the pictures which we have now look exactly like animals, and some of them even move like animals.

("al-Fataawa al-Qayyimah lil-Usrat al-Muslimah", Pages 169-170)

*Q*uestion: What is the ruling upon making dolls out of clay and then kneading it back into a formless lump?

Answer from Sheikh al-'Utheimeen, may Allaah have mercy upon him: Whoever makes something which competes with the creation of Allaah, then he is included in the meaning of the hadeeth, *{The Prophet, may Allaah's praise and salutations be upon him, cursed those who make pictures.}* (Bukharee 5038) And the hadeeth, *{The most severely punished people on the Day of Judgment are those who made pictures.}* (Bukhaaree 5613, Muslim 4030, Al-Haakim: 5235, at-Tirmidhi 335) However, if it is as you said, it is not a clear picture- meaning, it does not have eyes or nose or mouth or fingers- then this is not a complete picture and is not competing with the creation of Allaah.

("al-Fataawa al-Qayyimah lil-Usrat al-Muslimah", Page 206)

*Q*uestion: Many toys have hand-drawn pictures of living things with souls (such as animals and people); and the reason for this is usually teaching them, as in the speaking books (these are computerized toys which teach small children supplications or the like of that, and Allaah knows best).

Answer from Sheikh Muhammad ibn Saalih al-'Utheimeen, may Allaah have mercy upon him: If it is for entertaining the small children, then this is from that which is allowed for the children's toys- that which is similar to these pictures. And this is not prohibited because the figures in these pictures are not similar to that which Allaah created, as that which is in front of me makes clear (he was give an example of what the questioner was asking about). And this matter with this is some ease concerning the children.

If this is so, Esteemed Sheikh, if it is for the children then there is no problem, then why do we not say about the music which is in these toys, like the speaking book, which are aimed at the small children- is this also a case of ease because they are small?

The Sheikh went on to say, We cannot be easy concerning this aspect of music because there is no precedent from the Sunnah and because musical instruments have been prohibited in general- which is not the case with pictures. And if the child gets used to music, it will become something natural to him.

("Majmoo'at Asilah Tuhim al-Usra al-Muslimah" quoted in, "Tarbiyat al-Abnaa': Sawaal wa Jawaab" Pages 106-107)

*Q*uestion: What is the ruling on teaching the children with pictures and stories about animals and other things which have souls? And these stories are in books specifically for teaching the children, which have pictures in them of things which have souls.

Answer from Sheikh al-Albaani, may Allaah have mercy upon him: Making this generalization that it is permissible is not something praised, nor is it legislated.

("Silsilat al-Huda wa an-Noor", as quoted in "Tarbiyat al-Abnaa': Sawaal wa Jawaab" Page107)

*Q*uestion: What is the ruling on educating children with cartoons for the purpose of benefiting them and teaching them good manners?

Answer from Sheikh Fauzaan, may Allaah preserve him: Allaah made pictures of those things with souls forbidden, and it is forbidden to acquire them- so how can we teach our children upon them?? How can we educate them based upon something that is prohibited, upon pictures that are forbidden and drawings that move and speak and are similar to human beings? This is an evil picture and it is unlawful to educate children using it.

This is what the disbelievers want. They want us to

oppose what the Messenger of Allaah, may Allaah's praise and salutations be upon him, prohibited us from. And the Messenger, may Allaah's praise and salutations be upon him, prohibited us from pictures, and using them, and acquiring them. And those who spread cartoons amongst the youth and the Muslims, claiming that it is from teaching the children then this is an immoral education. And the correct education is to teach them what will benefit them in their religion and worldly affairs.

(Translated from transcription from the web site: Ajurry.com)

Question: What is the ruling on watching and buying "Islamic" animated-cartoon movies, given that these movies present purposeful and beneficial stories for children which promote good character, dutifulness to parents, honesty, offering the prayer regularly and the like. These animated movies are intended as good substitutes for television which has become widespread. However, the problem we face is related to the fact that such movies present hand-drawn pictures of humans and animals. Is it permissible to watch these animated cartoons? Please advise us. May Allah reward you with the best!

Answer from the Permanent Committee of Scholars in Saudi Arabia: It is not permissible to buy, sell or use cartoon movies, because they include pictures which are forbidden. Raising children should be done in ways that are Islamically acceptable with regard to teaching, disciplining, encouraging them to offer the prayer and taking good care of them. May Allah grant us success and may His praise and salutations be upon our Prophet Muhammad, his family and Companions

Question: In the curriculum of teaching in some of the schools the child is told to draw a picture of something with a soul or is given, for example, a picture of half a chicken and told to complete the rest, and he is sometimes asked to cut this picture into pieces and to put it back together again on a piece of paper, or he is given a picture and told to color it- so what is your opinion of this?

Answer from Sheikh Muhammad ibn Saalih al-'Utheimeen, may Allaah have mercy upon him: It is my opinion that this is not permissible (*haraam*) and should be prohibited. It is necessary that the ones who are in positions of authority in educational matters fulfill their trusts in this area by prohibiting these things. If they wanted to prove the intelligence of the student, they could say, "Draw a car or a tree" or something similar to that from that which is familiar to him. By this one can discover the extent of his intelligence and ability in various matters.

This is from that which the people have been tried with which comes from *Shaytaan*. As indeed, there is no difference to the child whether he draws a car or a tree or a castle, or a person. I believe that those in positions of authority should forbid these things. If they are compelled, they should draw an animal without a head.

Question: These pictures which are in books- is it necessary to erase them or otherwise obliterate them, and can the head be removed by drawing a line between it and the body, and does this change the prohibition?

Answer from Sheikh Muhammad ibn Saalih al-'Utheimeen, may Allaah have mercy upon him: I am of the opinion that it is not necessary to erase it completely because this is very difficult; and also the purpose of the book is not the picture itself- rather, it is to convey knowledge. And drawing a line between the neck and the body does not change the picture (so it is not sufficient to change it from being a forbidden picture) .

Question: The student may fail in school if he does not draw this picture in school. That is, he may not get a grade for the picture and then he will fail.

Answer from Sheikh Muhammad ibn Saalih al-'Utheimeen, **may Allaah have mercy upon him:** If it is like this, then the student is compelled to do this, and the sin is upon the one who ordered him and compelled him to do that thing. However I hope that the authorities will not reach such a state and force the servants of Allaah to disobey Allaah.

("Majmoo'at Asilah Tuhim al-Usra al-Muslimah" quoted in, "Tarbiyat al-Abnaa': Sawaal wa Jawaab" Pages 107-108)

The Use of Fictional Stories to Teach the Children

Question: Is it permissible for a person or individual to write stories from the imagination and everything that is in these stories is, in reality, just fabrications? However, they give them as stories to the children to read and to take lessons from.

Answer from The Permanent Committee of Scholars in **Saudi Arabia:** It is not allowed for the Muslim to write these lying stories. And the stories of the Qur'aan and the stories of the prophets and other than these from true events and that which narrate real happenings are sufficient for taking examples and morals from. And with Allaah is the success, and may Allaah's praise and salutations be upon our Prophet Muhammad, his family, and his companions.

("al- Fataawa al-Qayyimah lil-Usrat al-Muslimah", Pages 187-188)

Giving to One Child and not the Others

*Q*uestion: *Is it permissible for me to give one of my children that which I do not give another of them, because the other one is rich?*

*A*nswer from Sheikh 'Abdul 'Aziz bin Baaz, may Allaah have mercy upon him: It is not permissible for you to single out any of your children, whether male or female, with something while leaving out the other. Rather, it is obligatory upon you to have justice and fairness between them in regards to inheritance, or to avoid giving anything to any of them. The Prophet, may Allaah's praise and salutations be upon him, said, *{Fear Allaah, and be just between your children.}* (Its authenticity is agreed upon, and it is found in al-Bukhaari, 5/250, 2586, Muslim, 3/1242, 1623 and other than them)

However, if they are content with you singling out one of them with something, then there is no problem, as long as the ones who are content with this are mature and knowledgeable. Likewise, if there is from your children one who is unable to earn wages, due to illness or some sort of medical issue which does not allow him earn a salary, and he perhaps has no father or older brother who provides him, and there is no governmental stipend which allows him to fulfill his needs, then it is required that you provide for him enough to take care of his needs until Allaah causes him to be out of that situation.

("at-Tuhfat al-Baaziyyah fee al-Fataawa an-Nisaa'iyyah", Vol. 3, Page 227)

*Q*uestion: *If a parent has sons who live far from their parent and have less money than him, and other sons are living with their father, serving him, and under his command- is it allowed for their father to give the ones serving him some money during his lifetime or after his death due to their serving and staying with him? And, similarly, if he has more than one wife, and there is similar case to the above situation?*

*A*nswer from **The Permanent Committee of Scholars in Saudi Arabia**: It is permissible for the father to give to his children who have been at his service and attending to his affairs due to this service, as long as this is not showing preference to them over the other brothers. This is with the condition that that which he gives to them is similar to wages; whether that is daily, monthly or yearly. And the success is from Allaah, and may Allaah's praise and salutations be upon our Prophet, Muhammad, his family, and his companions.

("al-Fataawa al-Qayyimah lil-Usrat al-Muslimah", Pages 161-162)

Teaching the Children the Religion

*Q*uestion: *When should we begin teaching our children the religion?*

*A*nswer from **Sheikh Fauzaan, may Allaah preserve him**: Begin teaching the children when they reach the age of discernment; as beginning their learning in Islamic education is in accordance with the saying of the Prophet, may Allaah's praise and salutations be upon him, saying, *{Command your children with the prayer at the age of seven, and beat them concerning it when they are ten, and separate between them in their beds.}* (Hasan, Narrated in Ahmad, 2/180, 187, 6689,6756, and Abu Daawud, 490,496, from the hadeeth of 'Abdullah ibn 'Amr ibn al-'Aas by way of

'Amr ibn Shu'ayb from his father. It has been declared *saheeh* in "*al-'Irwah al-Ghaleel*", Number 2109).

As when the child has reached the age of discernment, then this is when his parents must teach him and educate him upon the good, by teaching him the Qur'aan, and that which is easy from the *ahaadeeth*, as well as teaching him the legislated rulings which are relevant to the age of this child, such as teaching him how to make *wudhoo* and *salaat*. And teach him the supplications for going to sleep, waking up, and eating and drinking, as when he has reached the age of discernment, then he understands that which he is commanded with and that which he is forbidden from. Likewise, forbid him from the matters which are not suitable or proper, making it clear to him that these matters are not permissible for him to perform- such as lying, backbiting, and other than that- so that he will be educated and raised upon the good, and upon staying away from evil from the time he is small. This is a very important matter, which some of the people are heedless of concerning their children.

Indeed, many of the people do not place importance upon the affairs of their children, do not steer them on the sound, correct course, but abandon them, neglected. They do not command them with the ritual prayer or guide them to that which is good. Instead, they bring them up upon ignorance and upon deeds which are not beneficial or good, and the those children associate with evil and badly behaved associates in the streets and neglect their lessons, and do other than that from the things which many of the young Muslims desire but which are from those things that are harmful. This is due to the negligence and heedlessness of their parents, who are guardians over them, as Allaah has charged them with taking care of their children.

The Prophet, may Allaah's praise and salutations be upon him, said, {*Command your children with the prayer at the age of seven, and beat them concerning it when they are ten, and separate between them in their beds.}* This is a command and an injunction to the parents, so the one who does not command his children with the prayer has disobeyed the Prophet, may Allaah's praise and salutations be upon him, and has committed that which is forbidden, and abandoned that which he has been commanded with, that which the Messenger of Allaah, may Allaah's praise and salutations be upon him, has enjoined upon him.

And he, may Allaah's praise and salutations be upon him, said, *{You are all shepherds, and are guardians over your charges.}* (al-Bukhaari 893, and Muslim, 4828) Some of the parents, and this is regrettable, are busy with worldly matters, and this is a great danger which is widespread in the Muslim lands- these Muslim societies deteriorate due to the lack of proper education and raising of their children, and so the result it that these societies are neither rectified or correct in the religion nor successful in worldly matters. And there is no power to change, nor strength except through Allaah, the Most High, the Most Great.

("al-Muntaqa" 5/297, as quoted in, "Qatf al-Azhaar al-Mutanaathirah min Fataawa al-Mar'at al-Muslimah", Page 816)

Question: How does a father teach his children at-tawheed (the singling out Allaah alone for worship)?

Answer from Sheikh al-'Utheimeen, may Allaah have mercy upon him: One teaches them *at-tawheed* just as one teaches them other than that from the matters of the religion. And from that which is the best in this category is the book *"Thalaathatu ul-Usool"* by Sheikh Muhammad ibn 'Abdul Wahaab; if they memorize it by heart and its meaning is explained to them in a way which is suitable for their understanding and intellects, much good will come of this. This is because it is built upon questions and answers and with clear, easy language- there is nothing complex in it.

Then show them things from the signs of Allaah which reinforce or demonstrate that which is mentioned in this small book; for example the sun- say, "Who is it who created it?" Refer to the moon, the stars, the night, the day, and say to them, "The sun- who is it who created it? Allaah. The moon? Allaah. The night? Allaah. The day? Allaah. Allaah, Glorified and Exalted is He, created all of them"- so that the tree of their natural disposition of Islaam is watered and nourished by that. Because mankind by itself is naturally disposed to singling out Allaah alone for worship, as the Prophet, may Allaah's praise and salutations be upon him, said, *{Every newborn is born upon the fitrah (the natural disposition towards Islaam) and his parents make him become a Jew, Christian, or Magian.}* (al-Bukhaari and Muslim)

Likewise, they must be taught *al-wudhoo* (purification for prayer): how one makes *al-wudhoo*, through action. One says, "*al-wudhoo* is done in this manner…" And he makes *al-wudhoo* in front of him. Likewise with the prayer- along with asking Allaah, the Most High, for assistance, and asking him, Glorified and Exalted is He, for guidance for them. And one must avoid all speech in front of them which differs from good Islamic manners, and every forbidden act, so that they do not become habituated to lying, deception, and bad behavior- even if one is afflicted with it. So that even if one wrongly smokes tobacco, he does not smoke it in front of his child; because they will become used to that behavior, and it will become easy for them to fall into it.

And one must know that everyone who is in charge of the house is responsible for the people who live inside, as He, Blessed is He, the Most High, says, *{Oh you who believe! Ward off yourselves and your families against a fire (Hell)…}*- (Surat at-Tahreem, From Ayat 6)

And it is not possible for us to ward the members of a household away from the Fire, except through accustoming them to good actions, and leaving off evil actions. The Messenger of Allaah, may Allaah's praise and salutations be upon him, affirmed this when he said, *{The man is the guardian over his family, and is responsible for his charges.}* (al-Bukhaari 893, and Muslim, 4828)

The father must know that his rectifying them is also a benefit for him himself in this world as well as the Hereafter, as the ones who are the closest to their fathers and mothers are the righteous people from both the males and the females: *{When one of the children of Aadam dies, his works are cut off except for one of three: the continuing charity, the beneficial knowledge, or a righteous child who supplicates for him}* (Muslim, from the hadeeth of Abi Hurairah, may Allaah be pleased with him, No. 1631)

We ask Allaah, the Most High, to assist us all concerning that which we carry of trust and responsibility.

(From "al-Fataawa al-Qayyimah lil-Usrat al-Muslimah", Pages 152-153)

*Q*uestion: *Some of the fathers have complained about their inability to raise their children. So what is the correct methodology in raising them?*

*A*nswer from Sheikh Muqbil ibn Haadee al-Waadi'ee, may Allaah have mercy upon him: The methodology of raising the children in the Sunnah starts from the very beginning. It is related in al-Bukhaari and Muslim, on Abi Hurairah, that the Prophet, may Allaah's praise and salutations be upon him, said, *{Every newborn is born upon the fitrah (the natural disposition towards Islaam) and his parents make him become a Jew, Christian, or Magian.}*

And in Saheeh Muslim, from the Prophet, may Allaah's praise and salutations be upon him, from that which he narrated from his Lord, *{Verily, I created my servants hunafaa' (upon tawheed) and then the Shaytaan caused* *them to stray.}*

Once the Prophet, may Allaah's praise and salutations be upon him, saw al-Hasan eating a date. So he took it from his mouth with his fingers and removed it from his mouth and said, *{Ukh. Ukh. Verily, I fear that it might be from the dates of sadaqa (charity).}* (al-Bukhaari and Muslim)

And in the two *saheeh*s, from the hadeeth of 'Umar ibn Abi Salamah, may Allaah be pleased with him, who said that he began to eat with the Messenger of Allaah, may Allaah's praise and salutations be upon him, and his hand heedlessly roamed about the dish. So the Prophet, may Allaah's praise and salutations be upon him, said, *{Oh young man, say "Bismillaah" and eat with your right hand, and eat from that which is closest to you.}*

In the *Sunnan* the Prophet, may Allaah's praise and salutations be upon him, said, *{Command your sons to pray when they are seven, and beat them concerning it when they are ten.}* Or a narration with that meaning. And it has two chains of narration which can be used for evidence for this matter.

And after that, also, you must be diligent in accustoming him to worship. But perhaps you might take your son to the *masjid* to accustom to worship and then we hear our elder brothers there saying only that they cause trouble or mischief by yelling- so they turn them out of and forbid them from the *masjid* using a weak hadeeth as a proof, which is narrated from Ibn Maajah from the narration Haarith ibn Nabhan, *{Keep your children and insane people away from your masaajid.}* Or a similar meaning- and this hadeeth is weak, as it has in its chain of narration Haarith ibn Nabhan, and his weakness is agreed upon. As the Prophet, may Allaah's praise and salutations be upon him, would bring children with him, and would not forbid them from being in the *masjid*. And in the *Saheeh* (al-Bukhaari), that the Prophet, may Allaah's praise and salutations be upon him, was praying, and his granddaughter Umaama was with him, and when he stood he held her, and when he wanted to make prostration, he put her down. And in the *Saheeh* also, that the Prophet, may Allaah's praise and salutations be upon him, said, *{I sometimes enter into salat and I would like to lengthen it, but I shorten it because I hear the crying of the child, out of mercy for its mother.}*

And in that which is *saheeh* also, and I mean here, in an authentic hadeeth, but this one is in the *Musnad* of Ahmad, that the Prophet, may Allaah's praise and salutations be upon him, was giving a *khutbah* on the *minbar*, and he saw al-Hasan and al-Husain entering and tripping on their new garments. So the Prophet, may Allaah's praise and salutations be upon him, left off his khutbah and picked them up and said, *{I saw my two grandsons and I was impatient because of them, and Allaah is Most Truthful when He says, "Your wealth and your children are only a trial…".}*

And in the *Saheeh* that Anas said, "I prayed when I was a young man, behind the Prophet, may Allaah's praise and salutations be upon him, and the old woman was behind us."

Ash-Shawkaani said that there is a proof in this that the child took a place in the row.

And the Prophet, may Allaah's praise and salutations be upon him, said, *{When the time for prayer comes, then the one of you who is most knowledgeable in Qur'aan should lead you in prayer.}* And 'Amr ibn Salamah said, "They found out that I knew the most Qur'aan among them, so I lead them in prayer when I was seven." (Bukharee 4062) So if his prayer is correct and he is seven, then he is allowed to pray in the row (with the men).

And yet the people treat the children in a repulsive manner. A child may have memorized a third of the Qur'aan, or half of the Qur'aan, or five parts of the Qur'aan, and then an ignorant old man comes and pulls him out of the row and makes him leave it!

My brothers, we must be established upon the Book of Allaah and the Sunnah of His Messenger, may Allaah's praise and salutations be upon him. And as for the hadeeth that the Prophet, may Allaah's praise and salutations be upon him and his family, would put the men in front, then the children, then the women- it is a weak hadeeth, as in its chain there is Shahr ibn Hawshab and there is a difference over whether the hadeeth of Shahr ibn Hawshab can be used as a proof. And the strongest opinion is that it is weak.

(From "al-Fataawa al-Qayyimah lil-Usrat al-Muslimah", Pages 150-152)

Physically Disciplining A Child

*Q**uestion: Esteemed Sheikh, it is permissible to strike the child if he makes a mistake when he is small? And is there some affect of this striking upon the child's psyche? And how is one to guide the child in this stage?*

Answer from Sheikh Muhammad ibn Saalih al-'Utheimeen, **may Allaah have mercy upon him**: If the child is taught or corrected through this striking, and there is no other choice (nothing else will correct him) then there is no harm in this. And this has become the custom of the people in regard to this.

If he is not going to be taught or corrected with this method, such as the child in the cradle yelling or crying and the mother hits him, for example – then this is not permissible. It is blameworthy, as in it there is no benefit.

The pivotal point concerning all of it is: Will the child be taught or corrected through this hitting, or will he not be taught or corrected?

And if it is the case that he will be corrected through it, then even then it is not a severe beating; for example, do not strike him in the face, or in a place which could kill him- he should be hit upon the back or shoulder or that which resembles them, from those parts which would not cause any damage.

Hitting the face is dangerous, because the face is the greatest area of honor and esteem from that which belongs to a person and the most precious thing upon the person, and if one is stricken upon it, he is humiliated and disgraced more so than when he is hit upon the back. Thus, it is forbidden to hit in the face. (From the hadeeth narrated from Abu Hurairah, may Allaah be pleased with him, in "*Saheeh Muslim*", No.6212)

(From, "Tarbiyat al-Abnaa': Sawaal wa Jawaab", Pages 39- 40. Originally from "al-Fataawa Noor 'ala ad-Darb")

Being Merciful towards the Children

Question: Concerning the meaning of hadeeth: It is related from Abi Hurairah, may Allaah be pleased with him, that the Prophet, may Allaah's praise and salutations be upon him, kissed al-Hassan ibn 'Ali, may Allaah be pleased with them both , and al-'Aqra ibn Haabis said to him, "I have ten children and I have never kissed any of them!" So the Messenger of Allaah, may Allaah's praise and salutations be upon him, said, {Whoever does not have mercy on the people, Allaah will not be merciful to him.} And this was related by the two Sheikhs (al-Bukhaari and Muslim)

Answer from Sheikh Muhammad ibn Saalih al-'Utheimeen, may Allaah have mercy upon him, who said,

{Whoever does not have mercy on the people, Allaah will not be merciful to him.} This means that the one who is not merciful to the people, Allaah, Glorified and Exalted, will not show mercy to him- and may Allaah protect us from that- and he will not be favored with mercy.

That is proof of the permissibility of kissing the

small children due to mercy and kindness- and this is whether the child is from your own offspring, or the children of your sons and daughters, or from those who are not related to you because this requires mercy, and that you have a heart which has mercy for the little ones. And the more mercy mankind shows to the servants of Allaah, the closer he is to Allaah's mercy. So much so that Allaah, Glorified and Exalted is He, forgave the woman who committed fornication; and He forgave her when she was merciful to a dog which was eating mud out of thirst. She went down a well and gave it water in her shoe and he drank it. She was merciful to the dog. However, if Allaah places in a person's heart mercy to these weak ones, than this is a proof that he will be forgiven or shown mercy to, if Allaah wills it. We ask Allaah to have mercy on us and you all.

The Prophet, may Allaah's praise and salutations be upon him, said, *{Whoever does not have mercy on the people, Allaah will not be merciful to him.}* This proves that it is necessary for a person to make his heart compassionate and merciful- and this is in opposition to what some of the fools amongst the people do. This is so much so that if a person's young son comes in when the man is in the coffee shop he scolds him and shoves him back- and this is a mistake!

And there is the Prophet, may Allaah's praise and salutations be upon him, who is the best of the people in manners, and the greatest of them in regards to character. There was a day when he was praying and while he was prostrating al-Hasan ibn 'Ali ibn Abi Taalib entered and climbed on his back while he was in prostration- like children do- and so he spent a long time in prostration. The companions were surprised and he said, *{My grandson made me into a riding animal, and I didn't want to stand up until his desire to do so was finished.}* ("*Musnad*" al Imaam Ahmad, Vol. 2, Page 513 and Haakim, Vol. 3, Page 127) And this was from mercy.

Another day, Umaama bint Zainab, the daughter of the daughter of the Messenger of Allaah, may Allaah's praise and salutations be upon him, who was small- the Messenger of Allaah, may Allaah's praise and salutations be upon him, took her to the *masjid*. He came forward and led the people in prayer while he was carrying the little girl. When he prostrated he put her down and when he stood up, he held her. All of this was from mercy and kindness for her. Otherwise, he could have said to 'Aishah or any of his other wives, "Take this girl!" But he felt merciful towards her because she wanted her grandfather- and he wanted her to be happy. ("*Saheeh al-Bukhaari*", Vol. 1, Page 131, from the hadeeth of Abi Qatadah al-Ansaaree)

And another day, he was giving the *Jumu'ah khutbah* and Hasan and Husayn were wearing new clothing which were too long. They kept walking on them and tripping, so he came down from the *minbar* and carried them both in front of him and said, *{Allaah told the truth when He said, ❁ Verily your wealth and children are a trial❁- (Surat at-Taghaabun, Ayat 15)}* (Saheeh al-Bukhaari) And he, may Allaah's praise and salutations be upon him, also said that he saw then tripping and he was not happy until he came down and carried them.

And that which is important is that we have to make ourselves love the children and be merciful towards them, and to be merciful towards anyone who needs mercy from the orphans, the poor people, the old people and others. Also, that we make our hearts merciful so that Allaah will forgive us and be merciful towards us- because we also need mercy and our mercy towards the servants of Allaah is a reason for Allaah's mercy towards us.

We ask Allaah to open His mercy for all of us.

("*Sharh Riyaadh as-Saaliheen*", under hadeeth number 893, From "*Tarbiyat al-Abnaa': Sawaal wa Jawaab*", Pages 28-29)

The Woman taking her Children to the Masjid

Question: What is the ruling concerning the woman taking her children to the masjid?

Answer from Sheikh Saalih ibn Fauzaan ibn 'Abdullah al-Fauzaan, may Allaah preserve him: Taking the children to the *masjid* is a matter which requires explanation and clarification. If the children are of the age of discernment, seven years old, then they should be taken to the *masjid* for the purpose of practicing the prayer, being educated in it, and their establishment of that which is obligatory. If they are less than seven years old, then they do not need to be taken to the *masjid*, in order that they not disturb the people who are praying, do harm to the *masjid* or dirty it. If it is possible to keep them under control, and it is necessary to take them, such as one fearing for them if they remain in the house, then it is permissible to do so.

("Naseehah wa Fatawaa Khaasat bil-Mara'at al-Muslimah", a collection of rulings and advices from Sheikh Fauzaan, Pages 41-42)

The Covering of the Parent from the Hellfire

Question: The Messenger of Allaah, may Allaah's praise and salutations be upon him, said, {The one who has three daughters with whom he is patient, and whom he gives them to drink and clothes them, they will be for him a covering from the Hellfire.} (al-Bukhaari, 3/332, 1418, 2/136, 8/8, Muslim, 40/2027, 2630, and other than them with similar wording) Is the covering from the Hellfire for their father only, or is the woman included in that? As I, may Allaah be praised, have three daughters.

Answer from Sheikh 'Abdul 'Aziz bin Baaz, may Allaah have mercy upon him: The hadeeth is general, including the father and the mother, with his, may Allaah's praise and salutations be upon him, saying, *{The one who has two daughters and treats them well, they will be for him a covering from the Hellfire.}* (see above). Likewise, if he has sisters, paternal or maternal aunts, or the like of these, and he is good to them, we hope for him by that he attains Paradise; as when he is good to them, then he has the right to a great reward due to that, he will be protected from the Hellfire- there will be a covering between him and the Hellfire due to his good actions. This is specific to the Muslims, as the Muslim, if he performs this good deed seeking the Face of Allaah, then that will be a cause for him to be saved from the Hellfire. And there are many reasons for protection from the Fire and entering Paradise, and it is necessary that the Believer perform as many of these actions as often as possible.

Islaam itself is the only foundation, and it is the principle reason for entering Paradise and being saved from the Hellfire. And there are actions that if the Muslim performs them, he will enter Paradise and be saved from the Hellfire. An example of this is providing for daughters or sisters, as treating them well is for him a covering from the Hellfire. Likewise, the one who has three young children (who have not reached puberty) die- this will be for him a protection from the Hellfire. It was said, "Oh Messenger of Allaah, and two?" And he answered, may Allaah's praise and salutations be upon him, *{And two.}* And he was not asked about one. (al-Bukhaari, 1248, and other than him, and it is an authentic hadeeth) Also, it has been authentically narrated that he, may Allaah's praise and salutations be upon him, said, *{Allaah, Glorified is He and Exalted, says, "None of my believing servants, if one who is beloved to him dies in this life, there is no reward for him except Paradise."}* (al-Bukhaari, 6424, and other than him, and it is authentic)

So He, Glorified and Exalted is He, has made clear that the true reward for the believing servant if one of his companions- meaning, his loved ones- from the people of this life dies and he is patient and satisfied with that, is the reward of Paradise. So a single young child falls under this hadeeth, if Allaah takes him, and causes him to die, and his mother and father are both patient and satisfied with this-then the reward for them is Paradise. This is a great favor from Allaah. Likewise the husband and wife, and the rest of the family and friends- if they are patient and content this will be a cause for them to be included in this hadeeth, along with their not having been affected by that which would prevent them from this, such as dying upon something from the major sins. We ask Allaah for security and righteousness.

("Majmoo' al-Fatawa wa Maqaalaat Mutanawa'" 4/375-376, and "Majalat al-Bahooth al-Islaamiyyah" 29/ 106-107, as quoted in "at-Tuhfat al-Baaziyyah fee al-Fataawa an-Nisaa'iyyah", Vol. 3, Pages 159- 161)

Question: What is the meaning of treating (the daughters) well as mentioned in the hadeeth (above)?

Answer from Sheikh 'Abdul 'Aziz bin Baaz, may Allaah have mercy upon him: *al-ihsaan* (goodness, good treatment) of the daughters and those who are like them, is through raising them and educating them with an Islamic upbringing, teaching them and bringing them up upon the truth, as well as adherence to and concern with their virtue and chastity, and keeping them far away from that which Allaah has forbidden of *at-tabaruj* (going out amongst strangers improperly covered or beautified) and other than it. Likewise, raising the sisters and the male children and other than them upon the manifestation of *al-ihsaan*, so that they are raised upon the way of obedience to Allaah and His Messenger, may Allaah's praise and salutations be upon him, and shunning that which Allaah has forbidden, and adhering to the truth of

Allaah, Glorified and Exalted is He. And along with that, he must know that that which is intended is not goodness concerning food, drink and clothing only; rather, what is intended is more general than that from treating them well in the matters of the religion and the worldly matters.

("Majmoo' al-Fataawa wa Maqaalaat Mutanawa'" 4/375-376, and "Majalat al-Bahooth al-Islaamiyyah" 29/ 106-107, as quoted in "at-Tuhfat al-Baaziyyah fee al-Fataawa an-Nisaa'iyyah", Vol. 3, Page 161)

Regarding the Child who does not Pray

Question: The questioner, who is a widow, states that she has a son who does not pray. She has advised and threatened him, but he does not care. He is sixteen years old. She says that she advises him, and he mocks her. Sometimes he does return and pray, and he says that ash-Shaytaan whispers above his head, and he says the like of this repeatedly. She says, indeed I seek refuge with Allaah, and I ask for you to assist me concerning that which is in him, and to guide me to that which is correct and what action this widow should take, and there is no power nor change except with Allaah, and she desires your help.

Answer from Sheikh 'Abdul 'Aziz ibn Baaz, may Allaah have mercy upon him: This young man who does not make his *salaat* consistently- it is obligatory that he be advised and directed towards that which is good, and that he be exhorted and warned away from Allaah's anger. Allaah, Exalted is He, the Most High, says, concerning the reality of the Hellfire,

❦ *"What has caused you to enter Hell?" They will say: "We were not of those who used to offer the salaat (prayers),"*❧ – (Surat al-Mudaththir, Ayats 42-43)

As abandoning the prayer is from the greatest causes for which one enters the Hellfire, as abandoning it is from the greater disbelief. The Prophet, may Allaah's praise and salutations be upon him, said, *{The covenant which is between us and them is the prayer, and the one who abandons it has committed disbelief.}* (Ibn Hibaan 1470, Al-Mustradrak 11, Ibn Maajah 1075, Tirmidhee 2612) And he, may Allaah's praise and salutations be upon him, also said, *{Between a man and associating others with Allaah and disbelief, is leaving off the prayer.}* (Muslim)

So the prayer is a very significant matter, and it is a pillar of Islaam, and it is from those things which distinguish the believer from the disbeliever. It is obligatory upon every responsible person, from the men and the women, to offer the prayers in their allotted times- and the child is commanded with it before he reaches puberty, so that he becomes accustomed to it and it becomes a habit with him. As the Prophet, may Allaah's praise and salutations be upon him, said, *{Command your children to make the salaat when they are seven years old, and beat them (if they do not make it) when they are ten, and separate them in their beds.}* (Hasan, Narrated in Ahmad, 2/180, 187, 6689,6756, and Abu Daawud, 490,496, from the hadeeth of 'Abdullah ibn 'Amr ibn al-'Aas by way of 'Amr ibn Shu'ayb from his father. It has been declared saheeh in *"al-'Irwah al-Ghaleel"*, Number 2109)

So also the young people. As for the one who has reached maturity, then it is obligatory upon him that he pray, and if he is late in performing his prayer, or falls behind in them, then it is obligatory that he repents. If he does not repent, then it is upon the governmental authorities who are in charge of such affairs to try him in a court and then, if this is called for, to issue an order or his execution, as the matter of the prayer is very significant, and it is the second pillar from the pillars of Islaam.

So it is upon you, sister in Islaam, to advise your son, and to strive persistently to guide him to that which is good, as well as warning him from the consequences of his evil action. If he persists in this, then disassociate yourself from him and ask him to leave you and stay away from you so that his affair does not cause damage or harm to you, and so that the punishment does not come to him while he is with you. It is obligatory upon him to obey your command, and to fear Allaah, Glorified is He, and Exalted, and to obey His command, Glorified is He, and the command of His Messenger, may Allaah's praise and salutations be upon him, concerning the performance of the prayer. So if he does not perform it, and persists upon his obstinacy and disbelief, then it is obligatory upon you to separate from him, and to dislike meeting with him, and to make clear this dislike and anger for him to his face, and to bring his affair to the one who is in charge of affairs from the governmental authorities.

And it is also upon you to tell those who are important to him from your close family, such as your father, older brother, or his uncles from his father's and mother's sides, to guide him and give him advice and punish him if they are able- as Allaah may eventually guide him through you efforts, in supplicating for him in your prayers and other than them, that he be rectified and guided, that Allaah guide him, and that he be inspired to that which is correct, and that he seeks refuge from the evil of his own self, and the evil of the *Shaytaan*, and from evil companionship, and that Allaah rectify him, and may Allaah grant him good...and from Allaah comes success.

(Originally from "Noor 'ala ad-Darb", Tape number 842, as collected in "at-Tuhfat al-Baaziyyah fee al-Fataawa an-Nisaa'iyyah", Vol. 1, Pages 306-307)

*Q*uestion: *What are the reasons for many of the young people turning away from the religion, and their alienation from it?*

Answer from Sheikh Bin Baaz, may Allaah have mercy upon him: There are many reasons for that which you have mentioned of the turning away of the youth and their alienation from anything that is related to the religion.

The most important is their paucity of knowledge, and their ignorance of the true reality of Islaam and its goodness, and giving no attention or concern to the Qur'aan. Also, there are few educators who have the knowledge and the ability to explain the truth of Islaam to the youth, making clear its goodness and clarifying its goals. There are other reasons as well, such as the general environment, radio and television programs, travels to outside the Kingdom of Saudi Arabia, mixing with the people from outside who have come here with corrupt beliefs, bad character and many levels of ignorance- and other than these, from the causes which are alienating them from Islaam and turning the towards godlessness and immorality.

For many of the youth, the emptiness of their hearts of beneficial knowledge and the correct beliefs, the coming of the flood of doubts and misconceptions, the misguiding calls, and the deceptive desires all come together and bring about that which you mention in the question- the turning away and alienation of many of the youth from all that is connected to Islaam.And how good is that which has been mentioned with this meaning:

Desire for her came to me before I had any experience

It met with an empty heart and was able to fill it

And that which is more eloquent, truthful, and better is that which Allaah, the Most High, says,

Have you (Oh Muhammad) seen him who has taken as his ilaah (god) his own vain desire? Would you then

be a wakeel (a disposer of his affairs or a watcher) over him? Or do you think that most of them hear or understand? They are only like cattle – nay, they are even farther astray from the Path (i.e. even worse than cattle). – (Surat al-Furqaan, Ayats 43-44)

I believe that the type of cure varies according to the type of specific illness they have. Yet the most important of these are:

- the concern and attention to the Qur'aan and the life of the Prophet, may Allaah's praise and salutations be upon him

-a righteous teacher, director and inspector

-the correct methodology (*minhaj*)

-rectification of the learning institutions in the Muslim countries and purifying them of that which they contain from the call to immorality and other types of godlessness and evil. And this will happen if the people who are responsible for them are truthful in calling to Islaam and sincerely desiring to guide the people and the youth to it.

-And from that (the cure): the concern with rectifying the environment and purifying it from that which has entered into it from disease.

-And also from the cure is not travelling outside (the Kingdom) except if there is a necessity for them to do so

- paying attention to the pure Islamic education through the educational system, the teachers, the callers to Islaam and the ones who deliver speeches

I ask Allaah for this, and that He rectify the leaders of the Muslims and make it easier for them to have knowledge of the religion and a strong connection to it, and to fight that which opposes it with truthfulness, sincerity, and ongoing effort. Verily, He is All Hearing and Close through His Knowledge. *(From "al-Fataawa al-Qayyimah lil-Usrat al-Muslimah", Pages 153-155)*

Review and Discussion Questions

Questions for rulings regarding the children

Review:

1. Why did the Prophet, may Allaah's praise and salutations be upon him, command us to have many children? Write the hadeeth which mentions this reason. (page 81)

2. To whom does the ultimate right of naming the child belong, the father or the mother? Why is it best that they agree on the name? (page 86)

3. Why is it not the same to feed the child formula instead of nursing her, according to Sheikh al-Albaani, may Allaah have mercy upon him. (page 88)

4. What are two ahaadeeth which indicate that images of things with souls are forbidden? (page 91)

5. When is it permissible to give to one child without giving to the others? (page 96)

6. What are some of the proofs that the parent is responsible for teaching the children the religion? (pages 97-98)

7. What are some ahaadeeth Sheikh Muqbil, may Allaah have mercy upon him, brings that deal directly with the raising and educating of the children from a young age? (page 101-103)

8. Bring examples from the Sunnah of the mercy showed to the children by the Messenger of Allaah, may Allaah's praise and salutations be upon him. (page 103)

9. What are some of the cures mentioned by Sheikh Bin Baaz, may Allaah have mercy upon him, for the illness the people turning away from Islaam? (page 112-113)

Discussion & Consideration:

10. What are some of the benefits, in this life and the next, of having many children, in contrast to one or two?

11. What sort of birth control was practiced at the time of the Messenger of Allaah, may Allaah's praise and salutations be upon him? Why is the encouraged more than the modern methods such as the birth control pill?

12. What two things does Sheikh al-'Utheimeen mention can be done to children's dolls to make them acceptable? Can you think of any other alternatives to these that you could suggest? (Hint: for some more ideas, look at Sheikh Fauzaan's ruling concerning this) Is it permissible for adults to collect dolls or keep toys like this? Why or why not?

13. How does educating our children with cartoons and the like fall under those things which please the disbelievers?

14. We should be easy on the children and not worry about teaching them Islaam until they are older. Is this statement true or false? Why?

15. How can we teach children about tawheed and other Islamic beliefs through example?

16. Is it permissible to hit a small child? How about an older one? Are there conditions ruling this? If so, what are they?

17. What are the benefits of treating the daughters well? What are some of the things that this entails?

18. How should we deal with a child that does not pray? Does this differ between the one who does not believe it is obligatory to pray and the one who is simply lazy? Explain.

Rulings Regarding

Other

Relationships

The Rights of the Parents and Keeping the Ties of Kinship

*Q*uestion: *Is the right of the mother greater than the right of the father?*

*A*nswer from Sheikh 'Abdul 'Aziz bin Baaz, may Allaah have mercy upon him: There is no doubt that the right of the mother is greater than the right of the father from many aspects. It is authentically narrated from the Messenger of Allaah, may Allaah's praise and salutations be upon him, that a questioner said, "Oh Messenger of Allaah, who of the people has the greatest right that I should treat them well?" He said, *{Your mother.}* He then asked, "Then who?", and he replied, *{Your mother.}* He asked, "Then who?" He replied, *{Your mother.}* He said, "Then who?" He said, *{Your father.}* (Muslim, 6665) And in another wording, the questioner asked, "Oh Messenger of Allaah, to whom must one be most dutiful?" He said, *{Your mother.}* He then asked, "Then who?", and he replied, *{Your mother.}* He asked again, "Then who?" He replied, *{Your mother.}* He said, "Then who?" He replied, *{Your father, then the closest relatives, then those next closest}* (Authentic, "*Saheeh Abi Daawud*", 5139)

("*Majmoo' al-Fataawa*", 8/309, as found in "Qatf al-Azhaar al-Mutanaathirah min Fataawa al-Mar'at al-Muslimah" Page 807)

*Q*uestion: *Who are the ones with whom one has ties of kinship and family relationship, as some of the people say that the husband's family are not from those to whom one has ties of kinship?*

*A*nswer from Sheikh 'Abdul 'Aziz bin Baaz, may Allaah have mercy upon him: The family members are the relations through lineage from both your mother and your father's sides. And they are the ones meant by

Allaah's, Glorified is He, most High, saying, ❦...*and the blood relations are near to one another in the decree ordained by Allaah.*❧- (Surat al-Anfaal, From Ayat 75 and al-Ahzaab, Ayat 6) And the closest of them are the fathers and mothers and grandparents and sons and grandchildren- this is ascending up the line or down the line. After them, the closest and then the next closest from the siblings and their children and their paternal aunts and uncles and their children, and the maternal aunts and uncles and their children.

And it is authentically narrated from the Prophet, may Allaah's praise and salutations be upon him, that he said to the one who asked, "Oh Messenger of Allaah, to whom must one be most dutiful?" He said, *{Your mother.}* He then asked, "Then who?", and he replied, *{Your mother.}* He asked again, "Then who?" He replied, *{Your mother.}* He said, "Then who?" He replied, *{Your father, then the closest relatives, then those next closest}* (Authentic, "*Saheeh Abi Daawud*", 5139)

As for the relations of the wife, then they are not the husband's relations, as they are not his relatives unless they are his blood relatives as well. However, they are the relatives of his children with her and Allaah is the Granter of Success.

("Fatawaa Islaamiyyah lil Musnad", 4/195, as quoted in "Qatf al-Azhaar al-Mutanaathirah min Fataawa al-Mar'at al-Muslimah" Pages 807-808)

*Q*uestion: *It is known that the wife is obligated to obey her husband, as is found in the hadeeth. She is also commanded with obedience to her parents in that which is not wrongdoing. What is the ruling when the two commands conflict- which of them is first in importance?*

*A*nswer from Sheikh Saalih ibn Fauzaan ibn 'Abdullah al-Fauzaan, may Allaah preserve him: There is no doubt that the woman is commanded to obey Allaah, Glorified is He, the Most High, as well as being commanded with obedience to her husband and her parents- and these last two are included in obedience to Allaah, Glorified and Exalted is He.

As for the obedience to the created, from the parent or husband, which contains wrongdoing to the Creator, then this is not permissible, due to his, may Allaah's praise and salutations be upon him, saying, *{Indeed, obedience is in that which is good.}* (Narrated by Imaam al-Bukhaari in his "*Saheeh*", 8/106, from the hadeeth of 'Ali ibn Abi Taalib, may Allaah be pleased with him)

Also his, may Allaah's praise and salutations be upon him, saying, *{There is no obedience to the created}* and this includes the parent or husband *{in disobedience to the Creator.}* (Ahmad 5/66, al-Haakim 3/123, al-Baghawi in "*Sharh as-Sunnah*", 10/44)

So if the husband is going to burden her with wrongdoing to her parents and disobedience to them, then she does not obey him in this; as the rights of the parents (in this case) are given priority over the rights of the husband. So if he seeks from her to disobey her parents, then she does not obey him in that, because disobedience is wrongdoing, from the greatest of the great sins after associating others with Allaah.

("Naseehah wa Fatawaa Khaasat bil-Mara'at al-Muslimah", a collection of rulings and advices from Sheikh Fauzaan, Page 83)

Concerning Companionship

*Q*uestion: *I am a young woman who dislikes backbiting and slander, and sometimes I find myself in a group of people who speak about the affairs of the people, and they enter into backbiting and slander. Inside myself I dislike and hate this, but I am very shy, and so I am not able to forbid them from that. Likewise, there is no place to get away from them. And Allaah knows that I wish to enter into discussing something else. Is there any sin upon me in sitting with them? And what is it obligatory that I do? May Allaah grant you success in that which has in it good for Islaam and the Muslims.*

Answer from Sheikh 'Abdul 'Aziz bin Baaz, may Allaah have mercy upon him: There is a sin upon you in that, unless you forbid that evil. And if they accept this from you, then all praise is due to Allaah, and if they do not, then it is obligatory upon you to separate yourself from them and leave off sitting with them, as Allaah, Glorified is He, Most High, says,

⸨*And when you (Muhammad) see those who engage in a false conversation about Our Verses (of the Qur'aan) by mocking at them, stay away from them till they turn to another topic. And if Shaytaan causes you to forget, then after the remembrance sit not you in the company of those people who are the dhaalimoon (polytheists and wrong doers).*⸩- (Surat al-An'aam, Ayat 68) And His, Glorified and Exalted is He, saying,

⸨*And it has already been revealed to you in the Book (this Qur'aan) that when you hear the Verses of Allaah being denied and mocked at, then sit not with them, until they engage in a talk other than that; (but if you stayed with them) certainly in that case you would be like them. Surely, Allaah will collect the hypocrites and disbelievers all together in Hell.*⸩- (Surat an-Nisaa', Ayat 140)

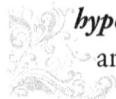

Also, there is the saying of the Prophet, may Allaah's praise and salutations be upon him, *{When one of you sees evil or wrongdoing, then he must change it with his hand. If he is unable to do this, then he must do so with his tongue. If he is not able to do that, then he must hate it in his heart, and that is the weakest of faith.}* (Muslim, 186) Imaam Muslim has collected this in his *"Saheeh"*; and the *ahaadeeth* and verses with this meaning are many. And Allaah is One who Possesses Success.

("Majmoo' al-Fataawa", 4/440, as quoted in "Qatf al-Azhaar al-Mutanaathirah min Fataawa al-Mar'at al-Muslimah" Page 856)

*Q**uestion: When should one employ leniency, and when should he resort to harshness in calling to Allaah and in dealing with the people?*

*A*nswer from Sheikh Rabee'a al-Madkhalee, may Allaah preserve him: The foundational principle in calling to Allaah is kindness, leniency, and wisdom- this is the basic foundation in it, may Allaah bless you. And if you encounter one who resists and does not accept the truth, and you establish the proofs upon him and he rejects them, then you put forth the refutation. So if you are a king, and the matter calls for it, then one must use the sword, as this calls for execution if one persists in spreading corruption. There are from the scholars those from various schools of thought who believe that this is the most severe evil, worse than highway robbery. So, one is advised, and then the proofs are established upon him. And if he turns away, then turn to a judge ruling by Islamic legislation for his punishment. This may be through putting him in prison, or through expulsion, or through execution, as it was judged that al-Jahm ibn Safwaan and other than him, and upon Bashr al-Muraysee, and upon, may Allaah bless you, other than them, that they be executed. From these are al-Ja'd ibn Durham. And this is the ruling of the scholars upon the ones who stubbornly oppose and persist in spreading their call to innovation. If there is benefit in this, and retraction (of the wrong which was put forth), then this is what is hoped for.

("Alhath 'ala al-Mawdati wa al-A'itilaaf" as quoted in, "Qatf al-Azhaar al-Mutanaathirah min Fataawa al-Mar'at al-Muslimah" page 67-68)

Concerning the Disbelievers

*Q*uestion: What is your opinion concerning keeping company with the disbelievers?

*A*nswer from Sheikh Muhammad ibn Saalih al-'Utheimeen, may Allaah have mercy upon him: If one desires through this companionship with the disbelievers that they embrace Islaam, and wishes to explain its virtues and benefits to them, then there is no problem with the people spending time in their company in order to call them to Islaam. However, if the people do not desire from these disbelievers that they embrace Islaam, then they should not keep company with them, due to that which their companionship causes, of falling into wrongdoing if the friendship brings about jealousy and affection; and perhaps it may bring about strong affection and love for these disbelievers. Allaah, Glorified is He, says,

❴*You will not find any people who believe in Allaah and the Last Day, making friendship with those who oppose Allaah and His Messenger, even though they were their fathers or their sons or their brothers or their kindred (people). For such He has written Faith in their hearts, and strengthened them with Rooh (proofs, light and true guidance) from Himself.*❵- (Surat al-Mujaadilah, From Ayat 22)

And having sincere affection for the enemies of Allaah, and loving and supporting them, is in opposition to that which is obligatory upon the Muslim, as Allaah, Glorified is He, Most Exalted, has forbidden that, as He states,

◊Oh you who believe! Take not the Jews and the Christians as auliyaa' (friends, protectors, helpers), they are but auliyaa' of each other. And if any amongst you takes them as auliyaa', then surely, he is one of them. Verily, Allaah guides not those people who are the Dhaalimoon (polytheists and wrong doers and unjust).◊– (Surat al-Maa'idah, Ayat 51)

And He, the Most High, says, *◊Oh you who believe! Take not My enemies and your enemies (i.e. disbelievers and polytheists) as friends, showing affection towards them, while they have disbelieved in what has come to you of the truth◊–* (Surat al-Mumtahanah, From Ayat 1)

There is no doubt that every disbeliever is an enemy of Allaah and of the Believers, as He, the Most High, says, *◊Whoever is an enemy to Allaah, His Angels, His Messengers, Jibraaeel and Mikaaeel, then verily, Allaah is an enemy to the disbelievers.◊–* (Surat al-Baqara, Ayat 98)

It is not proper for a Muslim to take the enemies of Allaah as companions, and to have affection and love for them, from that which is in that of great danger to his religion and his beliefs and way of life.

("Fataawa al-Mar'at al-Muslimah", a collection of rulings concerning women from various scholars, Page 595)

In Regards to the Internet Forums

*Q*uestion: *May Allaah grant you good; this is another question from the internet.*

Esteemed Sheikh, may Allaah prolong your life upon obedience to Him. We would like from you a clarification concerning the ruling of the woman participating in the Islamic internet forums- whether by writing articles, or responding to articles which were written by men. And is it permissible for her to speak to them in her responses with some of the statements of gratitude such as jazaakum Allaah Khairan, or other than that? And we would like from you the details of this matter, because some of the young men have said that it is not permissible for the woman to participate, and some of them state the opposite of that. Jazakum Allaahu Khairan.

Answer from Sheikh 'Abdul 'Aziz ar-Raajihee: There is no problem with the participation of a woman and her responding- as this is from calling to Allaah that she responds to the liars and clarifies the truth. However, this is with the condition that she does not put out her picture- she does not put out her picture. If she responds with writing then there is no problem with it, and she does not put out her picture. If she also uses an indicator of who she is or a symbol name without her actual name, then this is more proper, and if not, then there is no wrongdoing. And if there is no suspicion, doubt, or fear of *fitnah* for her, then there is no wrongdoing. And if she does not put out her picture, then there is no problem with her using name or using this symbol, and she responds to the liars, and clarifies the truth, with the condition that she not put forth her picture on the screen in front of the people. Also, her voice must not be heard. If she writes a message replying to untrue speech, and clarifying the truth, then this is from calling to Allaah- however, with the condition that her picture is not put out, or her voice, and it is preferable that she not put out her name---*and the speech is not clear on the phone connection...*

Review and Discussion Questions

Questions for Rulings regarding other relationships

Review:

1. What hadeeth is proof that the right of the mother over the child is greater than that of the father? (page 121)

2. What two verses are proof that we should not sit with the evil companions? (page 124)

3. List four verses which Sheikh al-'Utheimeen, may Allaah have mercy upon him, brings to show that we should not have great love for the disbelievers, nor should we take them as companions. (page 125-127)

Discussion & Consideration:

4. What should a woman do when the command of her husband conflicts with the command of her parents? Which should come first?

5. You go to a sister's house and the other women are engaging in evil or vain talk. What steps should you take when this occurs?

6. When should you employ leniency in dealing with the people, and when should you resort to a degree of harshness?

The Nakhlah Educational Series: Mission and Methodology (Pocket Edition)

Mission

The Purpose of the 'Nakhlah Educational Series' is to contribute to the present knowledge based efforts which enable Muslim individuals, families, and communities to understand and learn Islaam and then to develop within and truly live Islaam. Our commitment and goal is to contribute beneficial publications and works that:

Firstly, reflect the priority, message and methodology of all the prophets and messengers sent to humanity, meaning that single revealed message which embodies the very purpose of life, and of human creation. As Allaah the Most High has said,

We sent a Messenger to every nation ordering them that they should worship Allaah alone, obey Him and make their worship purely for Him, and that they should avoid everything worshipped besides Allaah. So from them there were those whom Allaah guided to His religion, and there were those who were unbelievers for whom misguidance was ordained. So travel through the land and see the destruction that befell those who denied the Messengers and disbelieved.–(Surah an-Nahl: 36)

Two Essential Foundations

Secondly, building upon the above foundation, our commitment is to contributing publications and works which reflect the inherited message and methodology of the acknowledged scholars of the many various branches of Sharee'ah knowledge who stood upon the straight path of preserved guidance in every century and time since the time of our Messenger, may Allaah's praise and salutations be upon him. These people of knowledge, who are the inheritors of the Final Messenger, have always adhered closely to the two revealed sources of guidance: the Book of Allaah and the Sunnah of the Messenger of Allaah- may Allaah's praise and salutations be upon him, upon the united consensus, standing with the body of guided Muslims in every century - preserving and transmitting the true religion generation after generation. Indeed the Messenger of Allaah, may Allaah's praise and salutations be upon him, informed us that, *{ A group of people amongst my Ummah will remain obedient to Allaah's orders. They will not be harmed by those who leave them nor by those who oppose them, until Allaah's command for the Last Day comes upon them while they remain on the right path. }* (Authentically narrated in Saheeh al-Bukhaaree).

The guiding scholar Sheikh Zayd al-Madkhalee, may Allaah protect him, stated in his writing, 'The Well Established Principles of the Way of the First Generations of Muslims: It's Enduring & Excellent Distinct Characteristics' that,

"From among these principles and characteristics is that the methodology of tasfeeyah -or clarification, and tarbeeyah -or education and cultivation- is clearly affirmed and established as a true way coming from the first three generations of Islaam, and is something well known to the people of true merit from among them, as is concluded by considering all the related evidence. What is intended by tasfeeyah, when referring to it generally, is clarifying that which is the truth from that which is falsehood, what is goodness from that which is harmful and corrupt, and when referring to its specific meanings it is distinguishing the noble Sunnah of the Prophet and the people of the Sunnah from those innovated matters brought into the religion and the people who are supporters of such innovations.

As for what is intended by tarbeeyah, it is calling all of the creation to take on the manners and embrace the excellent character invited to by that guidance revealed to them by their Lord through His worshiper and Messenger Muhammad, may Allaah's praise and salutations be upon him; so that they might have good character, manners, and behavior. As without this they cannot have a good life, nor can they put right their present condition or their final destination. And we seek refuge in Allaah from the evil of not being able to achieve that rectification."

Thus the methodology of the people of standing upon the Prophet's Sunnah, and proceeding upon the 'way of the believers' in every century is reflected in a focus and concern with these two essential matters: tasfeeyah or clarification of what is original, revealed message from the Lord of all the worlds, and tarbeeyah or education and raising of ourselves, our families, and our communities, and our lands upon what has been distinguished to be that true message and path.

Methodology:

The Roles of the Scholars & General Muslims In Raising the New Generation

The priority and focus of the 'Nakhlah Educational Series' is reflected within in the following statements of Sheikh al-Albaanee, may Allaah have mercy upon him:

"As for the other obligation, then I intend by this the education of the young generation upon Islaam purified from all of those impurities we have mentioned, giving them a correct Islamic education from their very earliest years, without any influence of a foreign, disbelieving education."

(Silsilat al-Hadeeth ad-Da'eefah, Introduction page 2.)

"...And since the Messenger of Allaah, may Allaah's praise and salutations be upon him, has indicated that the only cure to remove this state of humiliation that we find ourselves entrenched within, is truly returning back to the religion. Then it is clearly obligatory upon us - through the people of knowledge- to correctly and properly understand the religion in a way that conforms to the sources of the

Book of Allaah and the Sunnah, and that we educate and raise a new virtuous, righteous generation upon this."

(Clarification and Cultivation and the Need of the Muslims for Them)

It is essential in discussing our perspective upon this obligation of raising the new generation of Muslims, that we highlight and bring attention to a required pillar of these efforts as indicated by Sheikh al-Albaanee, may Allaah have mercy upon him, and others- in the golden words, "*through the people of knowledge*". Since something we commonly experience today is that many people have various incorrect understandings of the role that the scholars should have in the life of a Muslim, failing to understand the way in which they fulfill their position as the inheritors of the Messenger of Allaah, may Allaah's praise and salutations be upon him, and stand as those who preserve and enable us to practice the guidance of Islaam.   Similarly the guiding scholar Sheikh 'Abdul-'Azeez Ibn Baaz, may Allaah have mercy upon him, also emphasized this same overall responsibility:

"...It is also upon a Muslim that he struggles diligently in that which will place his worldly affairs in a good state, just as he must also strive in the correcting of his religious affairs and the affairs of his own family. As the people of his household have a significant right over him that he strive diligently in rectifying their affair and guiding them towards goodness, due to the statement of Allaah, the Most Exalted, ۞ **Oh you who believe! Save yourselves and your families Hellfire whose fuel is men and stones** ۞ *-(Surah at-Tahreem: 6)*

So it is upon you to strive to correct the affairs of the members of your family. This includes your wife, your children- both male and female- and such as your own brothers. This concerns all of the people in your family, meaning you should strive to teach them the religion, guiding and directing them, and warning them from those matters Allaah has prohibited for us. Because you are the one who is responsible for them as shown in the statement of the Prophet, may Allaah's praise and salutations be upon him, **{ Every one of you is a guardian, and responsible for what is in his custody. The ruler is a guardian of his subjects and responsible for them; a husband is a guardian of his family and is responsible for it; a lady is a guardian of her husband's house and is responsible for it, and a servant is a guardian of his master's property and is responsible for it....}** *Then the Messenger of Allaah, may Allaah's praise and salutations be upon him, continued to say,* **{...so all of you are guardians and are responsible for those under your authority.}** *(Authentically narrated in Saheeh al-Bukhaaree & Muslim)*

It is upon us to strive diligently in correcting the affairs of the members of our families, from the aspect of purifying their sincerity of intention for Allaah's sake alone in all of their deeds, and ensuring that they truthfully believe in and follow the Messenger of Allaah, may Allaah's praise and salutations be upon him, their fulfilling the prayer and the other obligations which Allaah the Most Exalted has commanded for us, as well as from the direction of distancing them from everything which Allaah has prohibited.

It is upon every single man and women to give advice to their families about the fulfillment of what is obligatory upon them. Certainly, it is upon the woman as well as upon the man to perform this. In this way our homes become corrected and rectified in regard to the most important and essential matters. Allaah said to His Prophet, may Allaah's praise and salutations be upon him, ﴿ **And enjoin the ritual prayers on your family...** ﴾ *(Surah Taha: 132) Similarly, Allaah the Most Exalted said to His prophet Ismaa'aeel,* ﴿ **And mention in the Book, Ismaa'aeel. Verily, he was true to what he promised, and he was a Messenger, and a Prophet. And he used to enjoin on his family and his people the ritual prayers and the obligatory charity, and his Lord was pleased with him.** ﴾ *-(Surah Maryam: 54-55)*

As such, it is only proper that we model ourselves after the prophets and the best of people, and be concerned with the state of the members of our households. Do not be neglectful of them, oh worshipper of Allaah! Regardless of whether it is concerning your wife, your mother, father, grandfather, grandmother, your brothers, or your children; it is upon you to strive diligently in correcting their state and condition..."

(Collection of Various Rulings and Statements- Sheikh 'Abdul-'Azeez Ibn 'Abdullah Ibn Baaz, Vol. 6, page 47)

Content & Structure:

We hope to contribute works which enable every striving Muslim who acknowledges the proper position of the scholars, to fulfill the recognized duty and obligation which lays upon each one of us to bring the light of Islaam into our own lives as individuals as well as into our homes and among our families. Towards this goal we are committed to developing educational publications and comprehensive educational curriculums -through cooperation with and based upon the works of the scholars of Islaam and the students of knowledge. Works which, with the assistance of Allaah, the Most High, we can utilize to educate and instruct ourselves, our families and our communities upon Islaam in both principle and practice. The publications and works of the Nakhlah Educational Series are divided into the following categories:

Basic: Ages 4- 6

Elementary: Ages 6-11

Secondary: Ages 11-14

High School: Ages 14- Young Adult

General: Young Adult –Adult

Supplementary: All Ages

Publications and works within these stated levels will, with the permission of Allaah, encompass different beneficial areas and subjects, and will be offered in every permissible form of media and medium. As certainly, as the guiding scholar Sheikh Saaleh Fauzaan al-Fauzaan, may Allaah preserve him, has stated,

"Beneficial knowledge is itself divided into two categories. Firstly is that knowledge which is tremendous in its benefit, as it benefits in this world and continues to benefit in the Hereafter. This is religious Sharee'ah knowledge. And secondly, that which is limited and restricted to matters related to the life of this world, such as learning the processes of manufacturing various goods. This is a category of knowledge related specifically to worldly affairs.

...As for the learning of worldly knowledge, such as knowledge of manufacturing, then it is legislated upon us collectively to learn whatever the Muslims have a need for. Yet If they do not have a need for this knowledge, then learning it is a neutral matter upon the condition that it does not compete with or displace any areas of Sharee'ah knowledge..."

("Explanations of the Mistakes of Some Writers"", Pages 10-12)

We ask Allaah, the most High to bless us with success in contributing to the many efforts of our Muslim brothers and sisters committed to raising themselves as individuals and the next generation of our children upon that Islaam which Allaah has perfected and chosen for us, and which He has enabled the guided Muslims to proceed upon in each and every century. We ask him to forgive us, and forgive the Muslim men and the Muslim women, and to guide all the believers to everything He loves and is pleased with. The success is from Allaah, The Most High The Most Exalted, alone and all praise is due to Him.

Abu Sukhailah Khalil Ibn-Abelahyi
Taalib al-Ilm Educational Resources

BOOK PUBLICATION PREVIEW:

Al-Waajibaat:
The Obligatory Matters

What it is Decreed that Every Male and Female Muslim Must Have Knowledge Of -from the statements of Sheikh al-Islaam Muhammad ibn 'Abdul-Wahaab

(A Step By Step Course on The Fundamental Beliefs of Islaam- with Lesson Questions, Quizzes, & Exams)

Collected and Arranged by Umm Mujaahid Khadijah Bint Lacina al-Amreekiyyah

[Available: **Now** - **Self Study/ Teachers Edition** price: (Soft cover) **$20** (Hard cover) **$27** **Directed Study Edition** price: **$17.50** - **Exercise Workbook** price: **$10** ¦ eBook **$9.99**]

SCAN WITH SMARTPHONE

FOR MORE INFORMATION

SCAN WITH SMARTPHONE

FOR MORE INFORMATION

BOOK PUBLICATION PREVIEW:

Statements of the Guiding Scholars of Our Age Regarding Books & their Advice to the Beginner Seeker of Knowledge

with Selections from the Following Scholars:
Sheikh 'Abdul-'Azeez ibn 'Abdullah ibn Baaz -Sheikh Muhammad ibn Saaleh al-'Utheimein - Sheikh Muhammad Naasiruddeen al-Albaanee - Sheikh Muqbil ibn Haadee al-Waada'ee - Sheikh 'Abdur-Rahman ibn Naaser as-Sa'adee - Sheikh Muhammad 'Amaan al-Jaamee - Sheikh Muhammad al-Ameen as-Shanqeetee - Sheikh Ahmad ibn Yahya an-Najmee & Sheikh Saaleh al-Fauzaan ibn 'Abdullah al-Fauzaan - Sheikh Saaleh ibn 'Abdul-'Azeez Aal-Sheikh - Sheikh Muhammad ibn 'Abdul-Wahhab al-Wasaabee -Permanent Committee to Scholastic Research & Issuing Of Islamic Rulings

With an introduction by: Sheikh Muhammad Ibn 'Abdullah al-Imaam
Collected and Translated by Abu Sukhailah Khalil Ibn-Abelahyi al-Amreekee

[Available: **Now** ¦ pages: 370+ ¦ price: (S) **$25**

(H) **$32** ¦ eBook **$9.99**]

SCAN WITH SMARTPHONE

PRINT

FOR MORE INFORMATION

SCAN WITH SMARTPHONE

EBOOK

FOR MORE INFORMATION

BOOK PUBLICATION PREVIEW:

Fasting from Alif to Yaa:

A Day by Day Guide to Making the Most of Ramadhaan

-Contains additional points of benefit to teach one how to live Islaam as a way of life
-Plus, stories of the Prophets and Messengers including activities for the whole family to enjoy and benefit from for each day of Ramadhaan. Some of the Prophets and Messengers covered include Aadam, Ibraaheem, Lut, Yusuf, Sulaymaan, Shu'ayb, Moosa, Zakariyyah, Muhammad, and more! -Recipes for foods enjoyed by Muslims around the world

By Umm Mujaahid Khadijah Bint Lacina al-Amreekiyyah as-Salafiyyah With Abu Hamzah Hudhaifah Ibn Khalil and Umm Usaamah Sukhailah Bint Khalil

|Available: **1433** -pages: **250+** ¦ price: (S) **$20** (H) **$27** ¦ eBook **$9.99**

SCAN WITH SMARTPHONE

PRINT

FOR MORE INFORMATION

SCAN WITH SMARTPHONE

EBOOK

FOR MORE INFORMATION

BOOK PUBLICATION PREVIEW:

My Hijaab, My Path

A Comprehensive Knowledge Based Compilation on Muslim Women's Role & Dress

Collected and Translated by
Umm Mujaahid Khadijah Bint Lacina
al-Amreekiyyah

{Available: **Now**¦ pages: **190+** ¦ price: (S) **$17.50**
(H) **$25** ¦ eBook **$9.99**

SCAN WITH SMARTPHONE

PRINT

FOR MORE INFORMATION

SCAN WITH SMARTPHONE

EBOOK

FOR MORE INFORMATION

BOOK PUBLICATION PREVIEW:

Thalaathatu al-Usool: The Three Fundamental Principles

A Step by Step Educational Course on Islaam
Based upon Commentaries of 'Thalaathatu al-Usool'
of Sheikh Muhammad ibn 'Abdul Wahaab
(may Allaah have mercy upon him)

Collected and Arranged by Umm Mujaahid
Khadijah Bint Lacina al-Amreekiyyah

Description:

*A complete course for the Believing men and women
who want to learn their religion from the ground
up, building a firm foundation upon which to base
their actions. This is the* **second** *in our* **Foundation
Series** *on Islamic beliefs and making them a reality
in your life, which began with* **"al-Waajibaat: The
Obligatory Matters"**.

|Available: **Now Self Study/ Teachers Edition** |
price: (Soft cover) **$22.50** (Hard cover) **$29.50**
Directed Study Edition price: (S) **$17.50**
Exercise Workbook price: (S) **$10** | eBook **$9.99**]

SCAN WITH SMARTPHONE

PRINT

FOR MORE INFORMATION

SCAN WITH SMARTPHONE

EBOOK

FOR MORE INFORMATION

BOOK PUBLICATION PREVIEW:

Whispers of Paradise (1): A Muslim Woman's Life Journal

An Islamic Daily Journal Which Encourages Reflection & Rectification

Collected and Edited by Taalib al-Ilm Educational Resources Development Staff

[Available: **Now** ¦ price: (Hard cover) **$32**]

[Elegantly designed edition is for the year 1434 / 2013]

12 Monthly calendar pages with beneficial quotations from Ibn Qayyim
Daily journal page based upon Islamic calendar (with corresponding C.E. dates)

SCAN WITH SMARTPHONE

PRINT

FOR MORE INFORMATION

BOOK PUBLICATION PREVIEW:

The Cure, The Explanation, The Clear Affair, & The Brilliantly Distinct Signpost

A Step by Step Educational Course on Islaam Based upon Commentaries of

'Usul as-Sunnah' of Imaam Ahmad

(may Allaah have mercy upon him)

Study of text divided into chapters formatted into multiple short lessons to facilitate learning . Each lesson has: evidence summary, lesson benefits, standard & review exercises 'Usul as-Sunnah' Arabic text & translation divided for easier memorization.

Compiled and Translated by:
Abu Sukhailah Khalil Ibn-Abelahyi

[Available: **TBA** ¦ price: **TBA** (Multi-volume) ¦ soft cover, hard cover, ebook]

SCAN WITH SMARTPHONE

PRINT

FOR MORE INFORMATION

SCAN WITH SMARTPHONE

EBOOK

FOR MORE INFORMATION